Angle
of Reflection

Angle
of Reflection

Marjorie Becker
Jeanette Clough
Dina Hardy
Paul Lieber
Sarah Maclay
Holaday Mason
Jim Natal
Jan Wesley
Brenda Yates
Mariano Zaro

ARCTOS PRESS

Book Layout and Design by Dina Hardy
Cover Design by Tania Baban Natal
Cover Photograph, *Poolside*, by Holaday Mason
    © Holaday Mason http://www.holadaymason.com

ISBN: 978-0- 9897847-1- 9
Library of Congress Control Number: 2016953039

Printed in the United States of America

Arctos Press
P.O. Box 401
Sausalito, CA 94966

www.arctospress.com

To those who have traveled with us
along the way, including:
Richard Beban, Kaaren Kitchell,
Beverly Lafontaine, Ken Fox,
Jamie O'Halloran, Amy Shroeder,
Anna Mortal, and, especially,
David St. John.

Table of Contents

Paul Lieber

Sarah Maclay

Holaday Mason

Jim Natal

Jan Wesley

Brenda Yates

Mariano Zaro

Acknowledgments

Introduction

David St. John

In the early summer of 1987, after having lived away from California for many years, I came to Los Angeles to teach poetry at The University of Southern California. I came with only a few connections to other poets here, but I knew of the Literary Arts Center *Beyond Baroque*, in Venice, and I'd had two poems appear in the very first issue of local journal *Bachy*, courtesy of Bill Mohr and Papa Bach's Bookstore, back in 1972. I'd grown up in the San Joaquin Valley and, like every kid who'd had enough of valley dust, I'd always wanted to live by the Pacific. So, when I moved from Baltimore, I rented my first apartment in Venice Beach pretty much on the basis of its location exactly between the ocean and Beyond Baroque. Over the next few years I was able to meet a number of poets whose names I'd known only from anthologies or poetry journals; then I met more at the readings I'd begun attending, not just at Beyond Baroque but all around the city. The readings were both charged and charming, and I loved them all. I especially loved discovering that there was already a wildly eclectic and vital community of poets writing sensational work in widely ranging styles. I felt entirely at home.

Some of the poets I began to meet knew each other from poetry workshops they'd taken together at a variety of places—in particular the Saturday workshop at Santa Monica's *Midnight Special* bookstore and from workshops at Beyond Baroque with John Harris and others. Many of them had gone on together to start up other workshops and, then, establish reading series at wonderful venues, such as the Venice institution the Rose Cafe. After I'd been part of the LA area literary arts community for a few years, half a dozen of these poets asked if I would consider leading a small weekly workshop. I had heard all of them read their poems at some point or another, and I knew how gifted they were. I said yes, and thus was born what one of the poets began to refer to as *The Monday Night Poetry Posse*, an astonishingly dedicated crew that met with me in a group of six-to-eight poets almost every Monday for many years.

I mention this history because it is important to understand that most of the exceptional poets included in *Angle of Reflection* had known each other for years before I ever met them—they had been writing and commenting on each other's poems and had already forged their own system of trust and community before I was lucky enough to join them. For me, it became less a formal workshop and more of a weekly conversation about poetry and poets, as well as an opportunity to offer my suggestions on particular poems they were writing. From the very first, the poets of *The Monday Poetry Posse* became my friends, and my life became richer.

It's been some years since I've been able to be part of these quite amazing workshops, though The Posse has continued to meet and to bring in new, appropriately deputized members as well. Wisely, in my view, they have also understood the ways a group anthology could go beyond a mere showcase of their writing. *Angle of Reflection* celebrates the remarkable poetry, longevity (20 years working together for some of them), and the depths of the bonds among the members of the group. This anthology is a tribute to the nurture such devotion to purpose provides. As some readers will be aware, the ten poets in this book have published gorgeous, moving collections of their own poems over the past couple of decades; some, too, have become respected teachers of creative writing and workshop leaders. Each has carved out for him-or-herself a powerful and individual style; each has developed, through the years, an incisive, mature, and complex poetic voice. And, I'm happy to report, each poet continues to evolve, to test new lyric waters, to challenge themselves and each other with new forms and language. Their work blazes with and without the accelerant of the group.

As I read through the pages of *Angle of Reflection*, I was thrilled to find some of my own all-time favorite poems here—as well as new and startling work—by each of the poets. Now that I have this anthology, with its generous selections of their work, I am reminded why I love poetry and also the poets who write it—it's the purity of that belief in art, in poetry, and the willingness to dedicate one's life to finding ways to bring that belief into the world, into language. My admiration for these poets is boundless. I invite you to share my deep love for these poets and these poems.

David St. John
Venice Beach
September, 2016

Marjorie Becker

Marjorie Becker is the author of *Setting the Virgin on Fire: Lázaro Cárdenas, Michoacán Peasants and the Redemption of the Mexican Revolution* (UC Press, 1996) and two poetry collections: *Body Bach* (2005) and *Piano Glass/Glass Piano* (2010), both from Tebot Bach.

A Yale-trained associate professor of Latin American history and English at USC and a fifth generation Macon, Georgia native, she learned Spanish in childhood, studied in Spain and served in the Peace Corps in rural Paraguay. She has received an array of awards, including a USC Mellon Mentoring Award, a Faculty Fulbright Research fellowship for Mexico, awards from the NEH and the AAUW, and she was honored as a runner-up in the second Beyond Baroque Poetry Contest. Her poems have been published in journals and anthologies such as *Runes*, *Spillway*, *51%*, *Chaparral*, *Askew*, *The Cape Rock*, *Hispanic American Historical Review*, *Rethinking History*, *Beyond the Lyric Moment*, *Desde Hong Kong: Poets in Conversation with Octavio Paz*, and *The Southern Poetry Anthology Volume V: Georgia*. She's currently at work on both a new poetry manuscript and a historical monograph entitled *Dancing on the Sun Stone: An Exploration of Mexican Women and the Gendered Politics of Octavio Paz*. marjoriebecker.com

Durham, 1980

Madrid: 1937: the heart
of Paz's "Sun Stone"
a man, a woman melding against hard earth,
naked against a plaza known in peace for incandescent coffee.
In '37 Paz's woman, his man worked against,
worked through time,
only language's shards,
only love,
and the Nazis used Spain to test their will,
while Paz's woman,
his man, loved open,
loved as if
no
body.

Then Dan said, "Woman,"
he said "Woman,
you teach me Paz by Durham night.
You feed me membrillo, work the quince paste
against hardening scrolls of bread,
your small hands fill my mouth.
We move toward fire,
I enter you on your floor,
this is not me,
the real me roams Israel,
your hands, they work my legs,
I take you to the bed,
this is not me, I never display,
and anyway, this is secondary,
I never allow,
but the taste of pomegranate between your legs,
I am weak above you,
your hands, they smell of pine,
your hands are golden spikes,
your hands are water,

today I'm someone else,
I count, I count your hours,
push you toward a center,
work your legs like corn meal,
whoever else you've loved,
whatever I've pretended,
I think to make you new,
know to make you me."

After I left you, Dan,
you prowled my diaries,
their tangled scratches,
coded allusions to another man,
to a man who liked my raw music, my helpless grunts.
you read them as denial:
what if Madrid '37 wasn't,
what if the woman opened her arms to a scavenger,
took his handful of wisteria pods filled with secret words,
what if Paz was wrong,
no Spanish Republicans,
no man on the plaza,
only a woman—
her open tongue a morgue.

          — In memory of Octavio Paz

The Man Who Danced Me in Spain

fed me squid,
oceans of sea life hand to mouth,
placed Mediterranean flowers
near my breasts, in my hair.
He sang, showed me a stray
topaz, an amethyst, said his life
was his restaurant, said he missed
Jews, said please,
but I was a virgin,
left him hot, aching, virginal.
Didn't you marry, I asked
after the Clara party,
and he said, again, again,
but he picked me up,
had a strength I somehow didn't expect,
my own bothers me, I hide it.
He was never fooled, picked me up,
we danced keen as railroad pitch,
the night train, the open wail,
the jelly jar, its silver top.
He unscrewed the jelly jar,
licked out the preserve,
the ancestral fruits, peaches,
muscadines, licking me closer
to the heart I once had, young,
swimming naked in green and blue
waters, pale light,
preposterous.

Body Bach

Know this now as we begin.
I am yours as I couldn't be.
Your tricks of light, air,
those wild waters.
Leave you? Would again, but girl,
for this kind of life, this somehow fit.

I couldn't listen well,
stumbled on though his voice was emerald,
his voice was deep. Jews have seen, done
everything, as we talked, I jumped ahead
to the island alone, no voice, no man knowing
not just that I fucked around, but that I kept him
from his deepest propagation.
He couldn't start babies,
sperm didn't work right,
but had he been able,
I would have stopped it,
hard, cold, on the ground,
underground, he suspected,
fucked me partly out of spite,
but mainly, it was our body Bach,
a long ability to withstand the seeming infinity
of minor keys, my breasts tight, harder,
a work up, a forest of pain, no foreplay,
its reverse. We both knew that prelude,
we wrote it together in the sweet cottage
of a former life, before I recognized
part of every prelude had to be thick, deep,
gulps of a certain liquid, it had to be, before I knew
the taste becomes me, no, we were content then
to come together, something about our plastic limbs
our views of loyalty, permitted such a cottage
full of river ferns, irises, he pressed iris whore petals

against my breasts, ate strawberries low,
frothy, but we didn't yet know
the role, our roles, we hadn't been shaken
away, and of course I went first,
this return would be based
on sorrow, buried sorrow,
sorrow that could not be answered.
The promise was, every time,
we worked together in ways most can't,
don't. Worked because of a long darkness,
he hit me some, his taste for blood,
we timed our cruelties, he told me
of recent women, he ate himself off me,
his heart remained tender, pained,
I was insatiable for ferns,
knew, too, when we fucked in a thick
bed of ferns, he would leave me
that night, though, was our return,
and we listened—a long river-less Bach,
and as we found each other,
I turned away.

Since Anything Can Always Always

In secret ways I have always and forever
and elsewhere I am composing
new trills, serenatas, howls
internal thought and punctuation
and outside,
right here,
through and with the gin,
with Angelo,
his Caribbean eyes,
skin blacker than the world's own depths,
he brought me that night
the 12th pair of wings
but it was the first I knew
and since my blouse was long forgotten
and since anything can always, always
he kissed my shoulders, my arms,
attached the wings coarsely,
lifted me,
and with no need to say
that he would then and again,
anything can always always
particularly in heat this palpable, dense,
particularly in blue, especially in green Caribbean waters,
in and through his symphony of ease, waiting,
without question . . .

Internal Hum

She began interspersing air, hours,
traipsing up to the open night roof
her hands, her memory supple—
with however many she fucked or tongued
or, out of sheerest persuasion,
listened to, seizing a melody,
not for her collection,
gilded amethyst and train tunes,
her renaissance, re-fabrication
of swamp blues and pain,
somehow in her legs,
the nights so long,
the train passed below
and the engineer bought a telescope
first to watch and later,
and she knew it would happen
but hid what she knew
from her conscious, straddled mind,
he stopped, made an iridescent ladder,
and another of wood,
clambered up on top,
but that was 67 days later.
The first 66,
she fabricated
dance steps,
steps based time after time
on some lonely man's internal, staggered hum,
perhaps a hymn,
a wet and broken hope.

Painless Tattoo of Song

After Amanda I felt there would be so little:
the flood of daily gardenias,
the ones Amanda placed with a fervor
known to the religious,
that world of succinct, definite Shechinah,
angel of pain and beautiful lust,
attached firmly
to shoulder, behind ears, near breasts,
to flood what had made Angelo
and Wayne possible in his duress,
yet it would be Peter who found me,
attached emeralds,
naked emeralds stronger,
more whole than desert light,
refused to use his upper body strength,
his peril below,
just attached a painless tattoo of song,
V'shamru, the train ballads,
the worn to a pulp world of kiss,
he knew what I needed, said it, held, held,
held and kneaded my tearful flesh,
found within an invisible crystal metronone
as I saved Amanda, again, again,
let Carlton enter and enter before the figs,
the feast of figs and belief,
and before any need for figs, for heat,
turn to her, to me, refusing
the maze of outdoor fig trees,
stopped and stayed, quiet this once,
as Peter took me under the figs,
in earliest, most blatant,
and trembling light.

Respect So Raw, So Real

That time of inkling, that time of grief
and open grandeur, perspiration
when Otis appeared and Arthur Conley,
to ponder whether singing started
between the breasts or at the harbor
but not until their sisters sang
did soul, its simmer, its simple sin
arrive, arrive, arrive.

His tricks undid the inner light

that fell the time he took my pound, my sight,
my sense of trees and stole my sugar, yes the pound,
the pint of breeze and spices too;

I made him pie or would have but he ate, then tasted,
took my worlds so low, ecstatic, then my words below,
he craved some sort of thrill and paid no bill

and wandered, wondered why I'd felt such luxuries
with other men, my open men,
my shy exquisite sky of men . . .

Notes on Coupling

The world went wanton the night that she,
yes she, wore silk so soft, so lush so languid
in its violet purple pink-drenched-soul
she dressed the part to please the Allmans
though in fact, they missed her heat,
her downtown beat to bad-boy banter
she'd expected them again, again, to sing.

A Dark Determined Still Untold

They climbed on high, they sang, they saw
the meaning as the makings as they made it
start and stop again as they on high defied
and rendered as they opened, ripened

rendered just the inkling, then the purpose
then the permanence, the way to strip, to start,
to stay, the deeply, darkly lustrous glance,
the meanings yes, they made the meaning still untold

they'd started sex and deepened it, the women
there that Macon night so naked and so needy
knew and shared the simplest sudden certain sound,
the dense intense, the providence, the open early

orchestra, the hottest hopeful share of hands,
of arms and early fruit, the women there,
the sex, the school defined, remembered
tickled taught and trembled in the bedroom breeze,

and rendered gender, rendered time and taught again,
just start, behold the people there so openly
as there they stopped and stayed a while and wondered how
they managed then again, again, to fashion

frolic, find, define the deepest declaration while
the inner silk, the open school, the stop me here
as I engender all the morning's meanings, make it clear
that she, no other, she again defined the workings,

and the wonder of pull it up and let it settle
down and still remember as she rendered fire
that she, Shasheila, no one else
defined, delivered, reconsidered all the seasons stopped

but one when she no other could or would
defy the dark determined inkling
say it here at last, define, oh say it yet again
desire . . .

Shawl

Her day inside she shuddered,
shivered, seized the warmth,
the bold illicit light her man had found,
sharing as though he felt that she,
and only she, yes only she
could wear such certain shelter.

Golden Morning, Golden Night

The children, oh my students found me
danced, because they knew my poems,

my sense of sea, its season and they saw me,
said my name and saw how easily, how eagerly

they said this, that I shared the sudden
mornings ripe as peach as pleas as claim

oh now so gone, undone, my father's
feeling frankly tender and attempting still this last

to tell me, trying still, beguiling me
in golden morning, golden night, the

air he breathed bequeathed besieged as tender
trembling telling as the time, the timbre

golden, golden, granting sorrow too a time,
a space, a circumstance, my students see

a certain sorrow so supreme and
certain I can think and only feel his

handsome hazel eyes, his hope for me,
his face, his face, the grandest world

ignited now, his harbor light, his grace.

— *In memory of Marvin Jerome ("Buddy") Becker*

Jeanette Clough

Jeanette Clough's most recent poetry collection, *Flourish*, was a finalist in the Seismicity (Otis College of Art and Design) and Blue Lynx (Eastern Washington University) book competitions. She is also author of two artist books, *Stone* and *Rx*. Awards include Pushcart nominations and a Commendation in the *Aesthetica* Creative Works competition (UK). She has edited for *Solo, A Journal of Poetry*, and reviewed for *Poetry International*. Among her journal credits are *Colorado Review*, *Denver Quarterly*, *The Laurel Review*, and *Levure Litteraire*.

A native of Paterson, N.J., she earned an M.A. from the University of Chicago, Division of the Humanities, and was an art librarian at the Getty Research Institute. Clough co-directed the Los Angeles Barnes & Noble and Rose Café poetry series, and was artist-in-residence at Joshua Tree National Park where she continues to teach outdoor poetry workshops.

Evocation

She must practice, away from the comforter,

the form letter, the PIN numbers and transfer,

as in delphinium. A beginning without end is vertigo.

There it is, bigger. Orange, like the fruit.

§

How she loves the small lines decorating her face.

An evening redness in the west is full of dry color

and the evocation of future memories. Especially at night,

discoveries repeat in the undesignated city.

Acoustic Rain

I am a tourist in a sculpture of sound. Part of the sculpture itself,
walking among sound that rises from the floor and suspends
from the ceiling.

I add these symbols of sound to the composition: letters
are musical notation.

An instrument needs someone to play it. To hear this composition,
read it out loud.

First
The rainforest in this room is drenched with sound.

Whenever someone enters or leaves, the resonance changes.

The instruments have no names.

Here, a hollow metal cylinder suspends from the ceiling by wires.
Duck underneath then straighten up so the sculpture surrounds
your head and shoulders.

Others on the outside cannot hear the same thing you hear
coming through the wires.

If I could wear your head awhile I would, but there is only room
for one at a time.

The skewed ampersand in the center of your brow –
a frown, vulnerability, a scrawled star.

These sounds are new. With practice I'll get better at
naming them. Can one make sense of sound, other than
the sense of sound itself?

There are no directions in this rainforest. No paths, either.
It is baffling, erotic, and lush.

Second
Here is a thin piece of metal. Set it vibrating.

The vibrations will travel to your inner ear
then flash outward in shades of bright yellow.

This is one way that light comes to the rainforest.

Light comes from all directions, not just from above.
When you figure this out, it's called enlightenment.

Those who spend a lot of time in the rainforest may start to flicker.

What is that clicking noise? The language of insects, amplified.
They have formed a band of shells, wings, & antennae.

The only instrument you can take in or out of the rainforest
is yourself. Bones are your personal instrument.

Here are boxes that when opened make sound. They are called
voice boxes. Each makes a different sound.

No one lives in the rainforest, but everything is alive.

The metal is alive. The wires are alive. The light, the sound,
and the insects.

There are no mirrors in the rainforest. In order to reflect,
you must go outside.

The rainforest is here all the time, but some never notice.
They look for it on the map, not realizing it is the map.

By now, everyone is pleasantly disoriented.

Rest your head sideways on this instrument, like the others are doing –
the ones who smile and sigh, whose eyelids are relaxed. Who breathe
softly and are very awake.

Next time you are outside the rainforest, see how many people
you can get to do this. Include yourself.

Third
The rainforest looks like sheets of sound moving through space.

If you don't know how to play an instrument, experiment awhile.

It may take help to figure things out. This is ok, since you are
seldom alone in the rainforest.

The rainforest has no story because the rainforest is always present.
Things happen in any order. It is always now.

I went for a walk in the rainforest. When I came out, it was the same
time as when I entered. Maybe a few seconds later.

Once outside, I read a book. Listened to the radio. Did laundry.

The rainforest was still there.

The first time I entered, my watch stopped. Second time, the face
fell off. Third time, the rainforest had moved and I did not find it.

If you lose track of time, it probably went into the rainforest.

The sound of time stays in the rainforest forever.

Fourth
It is impossible to give directions to the rainforest. Nevertheless, people find it. Once they are there, the way changes.

Breath has many friends.

No one gets lost in the rainforest. No one sings out of tune.

Everything in the rainforest communicates clearly. My wrist understands that insect. Our bodies are a sounding board.

The sound in my body & the sound in yours are very much the same. What comes out differs infinitely. This is the source of harmony.

Dimension loses its grip in the rainforest.

When you leave the rainforest, light reverses its direction.

You can move at whatever speed you desire.

After
I was happy to find the rainforest. It is noon.

There is light coming out of my fingertips.

Memory

Forgetting looks like a canyon on Mars.

The canyon is collapsing.

One expects noise, a record of vibrations.

No noise, no record,
except dust settling into valentine lace.

How to explain the tracery I keep?
Memory is a looking glass I must learn to walk through.

There was a girl who walked through mirrors.
An illustration shows her dissolving into glass.

On either side of the glass, pictures.

Do you believe what you see, or see what you believe?

The pictures and the glass are fragile,
their edges rearranging into the next scene

which does not yet exist. The present is hinged.

Quiet

Last night the windows shook with it,
shaking me asleep and awake.

Light makes a sound,

a kind of jingle in the day's throat

quietly, as a thicket of marble crosses
viewed from their uncarved side.

As a hundred-foot swell coming to shore
until it breaks

itself; whatever is under its lip.

A glass of water makes a sound like glance.

The windows shake with it:

eye movements, sheet-lightning,
the noise of will.

Salt

I choose salt, a common mineral unfit for jewelry.
Its ladder is fragile and vital, which other jewels are not.

Salt lives in the blood.
It does not care how it is seen

but cares a great deal how it is savored on the tongue.

I cannot live without you, jewel of choice.

I work myself into your skin so we will last together a long time,
older and tougher.

I adorn my body with salt. You comply,
an animal drawn to the lick.

Predators skirt the underbrush but we ignore them
because our hunger is more huge.

I wish to be nowhere but with the saltiness of you.

Letter from Atlantis 2

The first shudder split the continents.
They are still drifting. Islands, even when they wrap the edge
of a beloved mass, bending spinal coastlines
to fit another's curve.

Here is the reason for waves —
they are emissaries sent across the surface
with a code that always breaks but is not broken.
A huge and fearsome arc. I was caught in it once,

an adolescent bodysurfer slicing oncoming swells
sideways and usually winning. The waves
split around me and continued to shore
while I remained behind the break,
focused on the next piece of flexed horizon. Caught

in the comb of water pulling me through its teeth,
sending me around the full curl
then raking me into a gritty shoreline mix

of gravel and shells, the by-now-shallow lip of ocean
tightening out to sea, grinning.

Raga 6

I begin to discern different styles of carved
elephants and gods. These have four thick legs
with room underneath for a pedestal fifth. Here,
divinity's stone wrist has relaxed beyond nature.

A white elephant soars into a dream
and wraps itself, belly and legs, gently around my car.
Above me now, the white plumeria.

    I expect orchids and teak,
not this grove of star-blossoms
announced by emissary sweetness
into the moist air. Five creamy petals

thicken to a butter center, then
a thousand thousand times proliferate,
jostling into galaxies suspended overhead.

                  My head
reaches the Buddha's immense, crossed
shins. I could brush my cheek against the fingers
draped earthward and tipped with gold. His chest

fills with incense. I've seen it happen — when stones meditate,
they assume the shape of breath. Even the dullest pebble
can become the nipple erect on a god's soft breast.

Coloratura

The woman next to me in the concert hall does not remember anything for long. She can inhabit only a moment. It doesn't matter. Music is the same way. Her daughter fills in mama's blanks. *Is this your new house?* mama asks. *No*, says the daughter, *we come here to listen to music.* When the coloratura walks onstage in a flowing white gown with sparkly heart-shaped bodice and singing high notes the mother gasps, and gasps again two or three times when the soprano ascends yet another octave. The daughter seldom sees her so entranced and takes her mother's picture with the cell phone, making a flash during the concert. At intermission she apologizes. *I am mortified*, she says. *We hardly ever see her this way.* Mama spreads her hands and says, *Unmortify, unmortify. It is beautiful.*

Tracking

Noon casts no shadow. We make our own on ground the
color of pewter, raw silk, and curry. Your prints, ridged and
unique, point north. This is the kind of thing I would do,
head for the road and go 90 degrees the other direction. On
a bush, red evidence, and brittle orange in the dirt. Call us
on your cell. Promise to come back. You go beyond the
place where you should stop, your position transferred,
florid, scented with juniper berries soaked in tequila.
Our formations are wrong, we trample fragile shrubs,
lose and find you again parched, lacerated, burnt under a
column of shade. All of which may be reversed – night,
our shadows sharp on bright snow. You are seated behind
a rock we cannot yet see around, building a fire. It is we
who come, in need, to you.

Leaving Palm Springs

Hot blasts lift a scarf of dust,
and fault zones shift their ribs.

The ground sighs and rolls over,
restless as a desert saint

whose ridges and misalignments
are scourged bare.

At these bends in the road the earth's spine
slings back on itself like shoelaces

then with powdery softness goes forward, twined.

§

I like the look of the windmill bones
backlit by the gasoline sun.
All skeleton and no meat. My elbow

juts over the rolled-down car window,
knobbing at an important hinge.
Another knobbed bone at the wrist

makes the delicate transition to hand.
My cascading bones stay in the dark
doing their linear work, then splay at the end

into five stalks where one licked finger,
surely as thread pulled through a needle's eye,
reports the direction of every wind.

§

My staccato thoughts gap.
Again I fail the test of coherence

by assuming sense is a chain link fence
or that it buttons to the neck. Instead

a Hindu god's windmill arms circle completely
like my elbow fancies to proceed, whirling.

The desert's origami blue
folds around itself,
and matter is brought to the threshold.

The truth of windmills allows space
between the shafts. Solidity is illusion

viewed from a long way off.

§

The distance between this and the wind farm increases.

Take in the scenery, ignore the gloss.

Tonight when constellations rotate overhead
I'll connect their star-dots and ride them across the sky.

The stars perceive my weight, turn their heads
and nip. *Wake up. It isn't night at all.* Only dusk,

and I'm driving across white sand reflecting
windmills as if they stood in bright water. Mirage

is a desire is so strong
I create out of thin air what is not.

Here is emptiness. My bones and yours
are disposable, if ever we were here.

Here

We board a train. The train is going a different place
than the place we want to go.

At one point we look at each other, get off, and change tracks.

Here was a train going the wrong direction.

It turns out okay but takes longer than normal or expected.

Changing platforms turns me around.
A statement and its reverse are usually somewhat true.
I am swept into the backdraft of a train.

Eventually we arrive where we thought we would.

When we arrive, we see pictures.

A woman dressed in white waits on the platform. She stays very clean.

In a flash, everything is clear.

Let me be literal. Light travels fast
and I stay in my own slow space waiting it out.

While I wait, light traveling from another place arrives.

The light that went ahead arrives somewhere else.
The light that came from somewhere else
is here.

Dina Hardy

Dina Hardy—recipient of an MFA from the Iowa Writers' Workshop, a Stegner Fellowship from Stanford University, residencies in Spain and Wales, and a Pushcart Prize nomination—is the author of the chapbook *Selections from The World Book* (Convulsive Editions). Her work has appeared or is forthcoming in *Best New Poets*, *Black Warrior Review*, *Bennington Review*, *Pangyrus*, and *Typo*. She lives in Dubai, UAE.   www.dinahardy.com

[Elsewhere scrims of light]

Elsewhere scrims of light at dawn with thick bars between. How many squares as the sun purples setting fog? The room fills with smoke, & all the words of eyes obscured—this word: the last two years in highrise whiteout disconnected to earth. Here each breath a new sentence in the engine, like learning to walk again under forgotten colors of an Aphrodite sky. I wrap myself in the radiance of the day you taught me to do headstands on the mountaintop until flowers bloomed from the back of my skull, & fig leaves fell from blind bees' hives into clouds. In this moment of inversion, a lone drummer boy beat back Napoleon's army with a stick & stretched goatskin, & I am cradle-knot dwarf turned infinite-diagram giant.

[In the Natural History of Projection & Bone]

In the Natural History of Projection & Bone we build our homes in arctic mammoth tusks. To mark the entrance, an arm rises from the water in the wood. In the hand, a bouquet of three red balloons. The water never freezes, but the balloons change color with the seasons. Take note not to trip over the walking stick stuck in the center of the dining room, or its shadow we've painted on the floor. This is our sundial, how we know when to eat. Before each meal, we close our eyes in remembrance, & our bodies become full of need. Crystals form on the ceiling, our food. Once, in the future, I knew we would remember this harvest. Once, I gathered gravity in my skirt.

[Fallen black figs]

Fallen black figs against Mediterranean brick in split sections so the closed curtain of sepals spun around calyx collapse, expose secret scarlet inside the mysterious wall with purple slit fissure laid open to light. Spilled seed-pollens of simulacra from flowering sex—overripe in sun & heat—turn to feast for bees' tongues in honey sweet to make honey sweet—spurs in flesh, ready in surrender to the season. In symbol, why blame Eve for sewing leaves? For knowing nakedness as a wound to dress and undress. For saying I don't want you all the time. To say I don't want you all the time on my mind—or I want you in forgetfulness, in a longing to be broken by the strength of flames, be torn apart to ribbons. Blindfolds block out bruise blue dark autumn skies in somnambulism. I take you for the end of the year. I take you in the end of the year and the beginning of love—or its burst echo.

the magician's assistant

Heavy, flowing garments kept women from being magicians'
assistants until the end of the second war. Emancipation for all.
Here, wear these trousers. Climb into this box.

I climb into the box. Simplicity cubed—until the sound
of the saw. Love is such an illusion. The moment when the body
is divided by desire. Half in love, half not. Which half, crazy?
Ophelia wrapped the weight of fear for a love not returned
around her shoulders, slipped (ambiguous) into the water,
an aqueous solution. Slid under. Her billowing shroud,
& gowns & gowns & gowns in the currents. Wet black pixel hair.

Rue in the ruse that turned ruin (definite). I walk into the
waves. What parching madness, what weight this stone, in stones.
Love—heavier than any object when, with sleight of unseen hand,
replaces anxious secrets in hidden pockets.

On the Island of the Fire Eaters

have you heard about the Come-to-Jesus meeting?
All the truths will be told. Fess up.
Accept what has to be done to move forward. Jesus can't come,

he's drunk—we're drunk also.
Alcohol and flames, today's milk and Oreos.

My name is Law of Gravity.

You are Paranoid Fantasy.

The floor, orange sand, scorches our bare feet. Our fingers
stream through each other's hair,

we try to read one another's thoughts by Braille,
by brute force. By the time you get this
the coals will be cold, but that won't happen
until all the pottery has been written.

Heard melodies cause sweat, so turn it up.

Uh-huh.

In the distance, a storm boils. I count the number of seconds
between flash and thunder—it's getting closer,
the distance separating Jupiter's hands, north and south,
of course,
you know what this means.

We've never not known fire.
You tell me you've forgotten the smell of snow.

Your pipe is not soft.
We're not being careful—the cover,
it's torn off and we're striking everywhere.

On the Island of the Fire Eaters

we burn books and eat the embers.

Our island's defined by darkness—what we can't see isn't ours.

We believed once the world was quantitative
drew charts of seven circles—
You Are Here—the X of subject.

Of the elements, water is the most receptive,
but the memory in fire is strong
when it comes to crimes against Artemis.

We are appetite—we beg for food, for the word.

Is smoke in the hand worth a burning bush?

Leaves curl into flowers of ash—soy ink blazes purple
plastic dust jackets charbroil.

Our faces flash red from the heat of prose:

The screen door next to Charlie slams. He leans forward.
Blow my tears, he says.
Lacking a hat, Daisy May perishes in the desert.

We roast marshmallows over these published corpses—toxic.

We glow from this fodder, this fuel, we feed ourselves with
history, with geometry. We write our names above the flames
with sticks lit from borrowed light.

corona

i definitely made out with cliveowen
on a couch in a bar where i was
with our goth friends
and cliveowen
you're pissed because cliveowen is not you
we were drunk, also pissed
cliveowen is the sun
cliveowen has a mahogany accent
i say i miss you
you say what kind of name is clive

A Brief History of Razors and Shaving

The king of hearts does not have a mustache.
The simplest reason:

    He's the only king in the deck
who owns a razor.

        Correct: Shave in the direction of growth.

Replace the old cut-throat.   Peter the Great
taxed any man with a beard.
        Sun to Sat,
        somehow,
        vanity entered the picture.

Make good use of sharpened flint:

    primitive metal
    working against flesh.

Pushing safety-tab
pulls spring-loaded blade
for removal—
      pat pending,
      physical evidence required.

In the barber's hands (pliers, steel), skillful
at bloodletting, teeth pulling. Surgeons and nature
operate with max precision

    using Occam's razor   shave off rulers

      and the transformation of clocks. Desire
      is time mixed with memory—invention,
      from fire.

With burning twigs, cave men singed their whiskers,
quarter-inch stubble the best one could expect
without electricity, AA-batteries.

Gillette's family home burned in Chicago's famous flames;
he turned to sales.   A design from the carpenter's plane,
                    guarding the blade with wood, now the progress
                    of plastics guarantees protection against nicks and cuts.

          Emperor Hadrian grew a beard to cover his poor complexion.

          A man tried and convicted for wearing a false mustache to church
          —in Alabama,

this happened.

          In Kentucky, everyone is required to take a bath once a year.
          If done right, one can drown in 5 inches of water.

                    Wet area.
                    Produce lather.
                    Rinse.
                    Repeat.

The razor found in Tut's tomb was sharp enough
to shave dark shadows.
                              On his mind—suicide:
                              the simpler, the better.

His blade sharp and sharper still across a leather strop.

          Begin at the beginning   what is known:

The king of hearts does not have a mustache.

A Prediction

And in the same way ancient bricks don't hang in the sky
        without detection or prevention from fragile men
who spend their inflamed, unabridged days mixing mud
        with clay and a quarter-percent sand thus stolen
from ornamental hourglasses unsold in shuttered stores
        specializing in fully rigged Neolithic fishing ships
(no wonder the need for closure) and how these clots
        placed in tiny fires never reach the extreme heat of
the space-time continuum, so too our eyes behind our glasses
        don't see the dull growth of trees until the day
bulldozers come to lay groundwork for a pre-planned bypass
        that will link the previous three-hundred-and-sixty-four
with the next. On this day of concoctions, confections and
        a type of contentment that can only last twenty-four turns
of the vertical bulbs comes a desire to destroy the machine
        cast from the same material it casts: "let us make bricks,
and burn them thoroughly" to briefly stop the production
        of more bricks from bricks, so breaking
the perpetual passage of microwavable minutes. Perhaps
        this programmable date of binary numbers is the day
in which it will be said you are a man to be reckoned with.

Yours Is Everything

Hers is dedication to dead brother
Hers is exact weight and material
Yours is word as hammer you swing
into parallax light

Hers cliché to say cliché but cliché
His personal pronoun verb article noun
verb temporal clause
His is cut the first six
then another six
Yours is everything is cut petals
by quinary-colored insomnia knife

Hers and his are student
His and hers are popculture reference
Theirs are slang & song lyrics
Hers is woman is moon
His is rhetorical millisecond
His is not bad
Hers is lunch order lottery tickets
Yours is five syllable pixel afternoon
gathering sunflushed desires into
swandive ink bouquet

His is letter to someone famous
Hers a brand name
Look at them
Who they know
What they see
Yours is architecture in erasure
entire city apparition quicksilver life
Welcome

letters from the land of white pith helmets
& puggarees

When I press the desert to my temple my eyes become
decorative papers with a pair of maps etched by fog.
I am the marquis of loss. Perspective shifts around a clevis, still
the directory of this landscape remains in whiteout,
& my accoutrements are somewhat heavy.

Attempting to follow footprints of the lion is akin to tales
of coming terror & crystallography for beginners not to mention
these mysterious apparitions that disorient me:

- ships found by 36 anonymous gold cloaks
- dancing found by 16 very sad girls
- a workman arrives with bricks to fix the wall

Diagrams from the mechanical curator include depictions
of a brass cannon & clockwork village

> Figure A: a comparative study of progress
> Figure B: a comparative study of progress

My vehicle advances with such rapidity there is a sharp,
grinding report within the gears, apparently, the sun travels
southward above the clouds,
night—
     come now, as I fire the first shot into the blinding
warfare of the future.

please carry
the salt-encrusted
metadata in your pocket
until the evening explodes
into a prism of fractured
luminescence

Tomorrow, I'll climb a mountain
using a handaxe
& some peanut butter

If I don't
come back

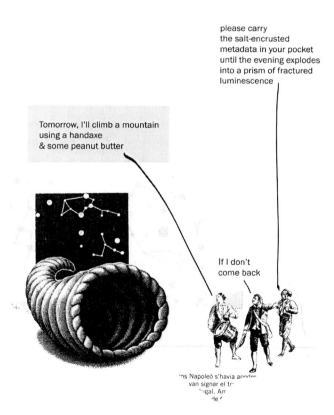

ᵒs Napoleó s'havia aꜞⁱᵒᵈᵉʳ
van signar el tr·
ᵗᵘgal. Arr
ᵈᵉ ꜞ

On the Island of the Fire Eaters

the flicker of death surrounds us. Projected on the wall at a party,
a group of guys—one's the party's host—stands around a cadaver:

a cinematic re-enactment of Rembrandt's *Anatomy Lesson, 1632*.
In the Dutch Golden Age painting, the dead man's arm is flayed,
muscles exposed for the lesson. We couldn't do that, says the host,
cut the corpse.

The dead man, now a dead woman in the movie—rigor mortis froze her
elbow bent, her wrist bent, her arm poised to make a shadow-puppet
of a swan.

I raise my drink to my lips; vodka numbs my muscles. The angle
of the body is wrong, the host explains.

The party makes it impossible to hear the film's director give orders
to the guys to take their places circling the naked, bloated woman.
One guy smiles into the camera. His cowboy hat, a stand-in
for the 17th-century doctor's hat, crooked.

Someone walks in front of the projector—his face, the screen,
obscures the image. He becomes his own light source, like Rembrandt's
stiff, illuminating us with his alcohol-induced wit and thick accent.

He's blurry. I'm tired.
It takes awhile to get to the door

...

the goodbyes, the kissing on the cheeks—three times—like they do it
in my country, says my host.

Dinwiddie   pg. 1996   Diphtheria

To build a life-like diorama, kill the bird first.

I grab the bent neck of a swan,
arrange artificial foliage, a hand-woven nest.

Paint and light complete the illusion

> of frozen mid-flight
> along The New River,
> purportedly the oldest river
> under thunderbolts.

Look through a small opening from a great distance
to safely view a total eclipse of the past,
a contagious disease in fission on a glass slide,
or what's framed in a transparent casket.

> On display in a department store window,
> five identical girls,
> ten identical shoes beneath
> matching sets of petticoats.

> Their lives began in incubators,
> continued on cobbled streets.

The hour before midnight a man passes,

> raises a lantern to their startled faces, says,
> I'm searching for someone honest, actual.

> He's partially serious; the sun cannot be contained
> or concealed in a box, cannot become the darkness
> of an uncharitable sky or your hand

over my eyes. If an orange is an orange
in a magician's palm and premises are true or false:

    —All birds speak French
    —Swans are birds, therefore, says the youth,
    —Swans speak French and will kill

or should be killed. If you were asked to deliver a letter
that would hasten the start of a war, would you
take a short cut or linger in the woods,
                    purposely become lost?

Your fever not high exactly,
but your pulse rapid as you count and pray upon

      a chain of poisonous berries plucked from vines
      at the river's shore.

How many swans have to die
to prove there's no song at the moment of death?

How come I can't stop making false forms,
can't tell the difference between a bird and a god?

Little Jesus

a large statue of a baby jesus
will make your house look small
even if it's christmas even if it's not
there are many missions in california
in los angeles I still haven't learned spanish
like a prayer forgive me
for taking the baby jesus for a ride
in my little red wagon if I were to talk
I'd say something wrong and wouldn't get home
I'd like to go you can bet on that
in this nativity scene the shepherd has lost
an arm the sheep are old and cracked

Paul Lieber

Paul's collection, *Chemical Tendencies*, published by Tebot Bach, was a finalist in the Main Street Rag poetry contest, and received an honorable mention in the Allen Ginsberg Contest. He produces and hosts *Why Poetry?* on KPFK radio in L.A. and Santa Barbara. Guests have included Poet Laureates, National Book Award Winners, and many other known and lesser-known poets. His poems have appeared in *The Moth*, *Solo*, *N.Y. Quarterly*, *Paterson Literary Review*, *Askew*, *Poemeleon*, *Alimentum*, and many other journals and anthologies.

Paul works as an actor and has performed on and off-Broadway and in numerous films and TV shows. He facilitates at the Beyond Baroque Poetry Workshop, and has worked as an adjunct Professor in Creative Writing at Loyola Marymount University, and lives in Venice CA.

www.paullieber.com.

Los Angeles

A car swerves in front
of the Mercedes in front
of me and the Mercedes
stops and I stop
but the car behind
slams my rear and
I hit the Mercedes
in the rear and we
all pull to the side
of the 101, 3/4 mile to the 110
going south at 6:45 PM
to exchange our dates of
birth and other intimacies.
The guy in the Mercedes tells me
he is attracted to men and
women. I tell him 25 years ago
my wife was crushed in a head-on
and I could only identify
her legs. The woman behind us
speaks Mandarin but cries
in that universal sob and
the registration whispers that
the Ford is not hers. I uncork
a bottle of Milagro
and we drink to our entanglement,
to the 101 freeway,
somber sips for the 40,000
a year killed in collisions.
We pay homage to that deer
mowed down on the 405,
to the possums that blended
with the 90, to the mangled
licensed and unlicensed dogs,
to mutts and pedigrees,

cats, squirrels, coyotes
and the seagull that couldn't
take flight fast enough.
The forty proof no longer burns
while the freeway ghosts
dance in the Santa Ana winds, then
relax on our dented hoods and fenders.
We hide the tequila and our mood
when the Highway Patrol arrives
in wool-blended shirts
though the temperature is 98.
We answer questions, thank them
for clearing the battlefield,
hug one another, deflate
our airbags and roll.

Aquarium

The blind acquaintance looks
out of a sound. I approach

his closeted face. There's a word
between rocks and a couple

of birds. A truck makes
a straight line of noise.

I blink like a street light, ask
what's going on? Shuffle

in my alley of sight. He answers
ahead of himself, talks of classes

he teaches, blackens me
with each thought. Each

student's name is chalk.
Fred, Eddie, Lila. I leave

without saying goodbye.

Off Broadway

Mike the director blames
Gilbert, and Leo will never
work with Gerald again, while
Gerald fixes his wig for an hour
and sighs about everything
but particularly complains
that Jack hits him too hard
in their kidding around
fight scene. Leo used to blame
Clarence, thought he would sink
the ship while Clarence
mocks Gerald, and both
he and Leo bet which inanity
Gerald will say when he returns
to the dressing room after
Act One. Steven thinks Clarence
is a horrible actor though Leo
argues he's improving.
Jack is homophobic
so detests Gilbert who sings
show tunes backstage though
the play we are performing
is serious and everyone
watches out for Tanya, who
is capable of ripping your balls
off on stage. She behaves
but secretly complains to Dorothy,
the producer, about Mike.
Mike asks me to stand by him
when the shit flies, while
Stuart, the other producer,
wants to fire Tanya, but Dorothy
believes in her. Stuart
loves me and gives me free tickets

but I can't tell Gilbert, Leo
Tanya, Gerald, Steven or Clarence.
The Times hates the play but
likes me, Steven and Leo, so
the show closes even though
Joanne Woodward loves it
and everyone except for Gerald.

Problem on Stage

She says, "move forward
not side to side, stand straight
I'll come to you," and I ask
how about when I kiss your neck
and she answers, "just bend,
as long as you're lower."
The next day I receive a note
from the stage manager
to keep my mouth closed
when I kiss her although I thought
it was, but I might have
moved from side to side.
The word from another producer
is she's really upset and that
this producer is being pressured
by the other producer
for me to keep my mouth closed,
but this actress has always been difficult
and when she pulls away
from the osculation scene
out of loyalty to my wife although
in the scene before, my wife
says it's okay for us to make love,
when she brakes and breaks away,
I lean on the counter and wait
for her next line which is marinating
in her stomach area, spiraling
up her esophagus as it churns
and churns and by the time
sounds form words and they
are released through her open lips
they've lost all logic,
all semblance of meaning,
but in fairness they are personal enough

and I'm thinking Lee Strasberg lives,
although he too was misunderstood.
And the knowledge that her actual
sister is homeless and an addict
no longer rouses my sympathy
when she withdraws from
the closed lips of my character,
the lips her character
is supposed to find irresistible.

Sum

There's her pale clear skin
covering the skull of another
who even wears her hair length,
the crouch, the bend in her spine
at the same angle.
It's odd to see the bone
in the bridge of her nose
displayed by this boy.
Such concentration in focus
in the corner of the café, by
the dark haired, falcon-like girl
with her visage glued to the screen,
considering and reconsidering.
It's her focus, yes. I'll never find
her impression of anything,
the one that changed
the thing she described into
the thing she described,
like Brando in the car scene
with Steiger, how Steiger's
choice diminished him
while Brando's made him
larger. Listen for her accent,
Russian mixed with German
and English in a delicate rasp.
Listen to her legs. Find them
on this teenager skipping
in front of you. Where are
her eyes?

The First Blackout

The subway stopped. I was
midway up the stairs
and without blinking, lights faded
and the sky joined Union Square.
I headed to 134 East 17th
climbed five flights and how my father
showed up at the draftsman-kitchen-
table I don't remember, but there
he was as if to remind me he
was still my father and though
his role seemed as arbitrary,
as, say, the unlit street lights,
he asserted, so it seemed,
that he was mobile and could appear
even after I had moved out,
even when transportation failed.
He brought his father fumes into
my incipient-bohemian-exposed-brick-flat
in his pin-striped almost solid
blue suit and solid tie, the one
my mother picked out.
He sat so comfortably and mocked
my neighbor who was mesmerized
by the Big Dipper also suddenly appearing.
How could his priorities be so perverse
as to put aesthetics before the
unexplained blackout that will cause
profound loss or signal an invasion.
It brought together unlikely clusters
in elevators, subway cars and in my apartment.
I'd lie if I said I didn't want him
there in candlelight.
I'd lie if I said I didn't want
him there, with me—
together,
together and helpless.

Encounter at the Market

Ed is less his prostate, unnoticeable
from this point of view while
prostates disappear like tonsils
in the 50s. Dave's is gone, Brian's soon
to be, Chuck's is under surveillance and
mine, age-appropriately enlarged.
We look through our prostate lens at the map
of urinals, Starbucks on Wilshire, Whole Foods
on National, while the empty coffee cup
waits graciously on the dashboard.
There goes Alan off a prostate cliff as Chris
drowns under four trickles of urine.
I inhale deeply, balancing between
the here and hereafter, between a doctor's
pronouncement and saw palmetto capsules.
Ed says if he knew how long sex
would be out, although none of those important
nerve endings were tampered with,
he would have opted for radiation instead,
and I can't help but visualize
him and his wife. Or is it the girl
in the aisle whom he refers to
as his eyes follow her past
pasta and dried fruit,
shrunken apricots and mangoes
withering alongside linguini
before it's boiled, still stiff
and on sale for half price.

I Just Spoke to Philip

and he was true to reviews,
no frills, polite and compassionate.
He'll pick up the body, burn it,
ship the ashes, and $575
caps the deal and my mother
whose thoughts, so confused
amidst themselves and reality,
but isn't that true for all of us,
but not Philip who offers
his rehearsed, simple style.
His phone picks up messages
24 hours and I, the soon to be
grieving son, or you, the grieving
whomever, don't have to think,
just charge it to MasterCard
and the ashes will arrive 7-10 days later.
I'll take hers past security,
scatter them in Thomkins Square Park
where they'll blow into the lips
of hipsters, the dot.com crowd might
get a taste across the bustling
Lower East Side that no longer exists
except in burnt and buried memories.
Someone once told me all colds are
the result of a loss as I burn
through a dozen tissues.
And what's the remedy? Cry, cry
for one you can barely listen to,
for conversations you never had,
for impossibilities, paranoia,
persecutions and all the anti-Semitism
that found her sharp jaw, brown eye
and blue, cream skin, her frail
and voluptuous body and
for all the hidden mikes
that couldn't trace her whispers.

Another Ocean Poem

I called you "God,"
not even a manifestation.
I called you "God,"
a blurt, a slip,
an innocent mistake
and you,
a solution,
a wet link,
a churning sway,
a swan, a flirtatious
swing on shore,
a flare of white,
a slide of your wing,
an approach, a retreat,
a beckoning.
I called you "God"
as if you weren't elusive,
as if you were the writer,
not the first page
or the cover, the binding.
I called you "God"
because I can't grasp
indifference, enormity,
frivolity and on and on,
as primitive as the beat
of every heart,
as complex.

Navy

It rained last night. It's as clear as
1950 when I had pink skin and hadn't yet
daydreamed murders. The hard lines
of Catalina can be traced, and the cliffs
behind me so defined each fold begs to be
named and you reflect a triangle of light,
your blue so dark, my mother would have
called you navy when she could see. You're
post-storm, twitching with mini-waves
scratching the shore. You had a difficult
night of water bruises. I'm so tired of
pricking myself. You ask why I keep
returning, breathing waves.

My Father's Cousins, the Ones I Never Met

Yes, you can personify the vast blue.
Here they come again, barreling

over one another, twins, cousins—almost
identical, *hardly* identical—they spread across,

keep spreading, a series of curls, then rupture . . .
Just as I become familiar with the bulge of blue,

it collapses. And ten strangers appear.
The seagulls pick the sand . . . A black-banded

one approaches, nonchalantly waits
as I reach into my pocket to hand her

a quarter. She backs off as if insulted,
but it's all the change I have.

Fluff white smooth stuff, she
struts as if she'll live forever; stops,

looks closer, asks, "What makes me me,
and you, you?" I tell her to read Spinoza.

An overweight seagull swivels his head
towards me, then the water. He squeals

like my son, strolls on twig legs, gains
momentum, then he's in the clouds.

A family of four waves, hurries to their
destruction. A family of three tips in, crumbles,

and the ocean, with its balconies,
rolls its tiers in a dreary narrative,

a repetitive tragedy. Another lush,
uninhibited file ends in a liquid flare . . .

Now sleep, yoga, a blue golf course
with no players. It's the rhythm

of your breathing, so they say.
It's really death slapping the shore.

And what about my heart that sped
at 165 beats for a loveless hour?

They attached a monitor to measure
the surf in my veins. The doctor

said, "It's not life-threatening."
He didn't know we were already dead,

breaking his news like a wave
spilling over itself.

This Is Not Jalama Beach

The clouds roll, swollen and stained
with eternity scribbled
on their stomachs.
I jog into one, speckled
with a breeze, this hill
covered with stubs,
and the ground,
a splattering of pebbles.
You were molten,
now a chill, the layers
of sandstone that some
might think measure,
but there's nothing
to measure. An abrupt
entry into the beginning
of angles, of smoothness,
of inhales, of edges
and shards. A nameless bird
on stilts, the breakage,
your crisp water voice
and my layer of skin,
all born at the same moment.
It's a primordial cut,
a slice of a planet,
rock tissue, the intestines of bone,
a carving from my brain,
the desert by the sea.
You've captured me with long streams,
with your ocean stuff
and my flimsy narratives.
A train of clouds, of waves.
My tumble of words,
my misfires and your exactness
pair up for a moment.
An audience of rocks.
The applause of surf.

Homesick

I'm facing north,
the ocean over my left shoulder.
That would be the Pacific.
On the east coast, the Atlantic
would be swaying over
my right shoulder.
Two blocks away my wife and child
argue and another 2448 miles east
stands Parker Jewish Memorial
Nursing home where my mother
free associates.
I skim the ocean, its swells,
channels and salutations.
The surfers look for thrills.
I'm just looking. They wait
for the wave in hiding.
Everything below the surface
rises and bursts open,
a billion epiphanies.
Where will they break?
Surfers misjudge the future
like the rest of us
as cells collect and spin in their
assignments; water cells
adhere to water while humans
stick to humans until
these smooth collisions.
Foam spreads,
temporary maps dissolve.
I sit cross-legged
and my calves tingle, asleep
until I change positions,
maybe move back east
and wake the entire body.

Sarah Maclay

Sarah Maclay is the author of *Music for the Black Room* (2011), *The White Bride* (2008), and *Whore* (2004), all from U of Tampa Press, as well as three chapbooks and "Fugue States Coming Down the Hall" (in *Scenarios: Scripts to Perform*). A 2016 COLA (City of LA) Master Artist Fellow, and a recipient of a 2015 residency at Yaddo, she has also received a Pushcart Special Mention and the Tampa Review Prize for Poetry, among other awards and fellowships. Her poems and criticism have appeared widely, in spots such as *The American Poetry Review*, *The Writer's Chronicle*, *FIELD*, *Ploughshares*, *The Best American Erotic Poetry: From 1800 to the Present*, and *Poetry International*, where she served as Book Review Editor for a decade. A native of Montana, with degrees from Oberlin and VCFA, she lives in Venice, California, teaches creative writing and literature at LMU, conducts Mini-Master Classes at Beyond Baroque, and served as Artistic Director for The 3rd Area, a reading series at the galleries Pharmaka (DTLA) and Frank Pictures (Bergamot Station). In October 2016, What Books Press published *The "She" Series: A Venice Correspondence*, her braided collaboration with poet Holaday Mason.

http://cola2016.lamag.org/sarah_maclay.html

Night Text

Let's imagine I'm translating something to you—
you, asleep, or sleepless or naming
that third place—between—

with the tips of your tapering fingers—

I don't know the language.
It bends.

In the mind—in that strangely shared chamber—
that is, I mean, in your hands,

where you show me those scenes of confusion and flight
with such intimacy, and don't know it—

even *sans* color, *sans* liquor, *sans* shape,
we are twins. Fraternal. Unknown.

The moon, invasive, huge,
lunging in through the windows,
makes no exceptions—

It's true: it will never happen / you'd be surprised.

28

There was her method of swooning, which involved letting go on an
ice rink of shattered glass, her long red hair strewn over the crackles,
cheek bones against ice cube pebbles (in their sharpness, like a mirror)
and the sense that below the ice glass or glass ice was another room
that could be looked into, or looked up from. At around the same time,
she noticed more men staring at her in the grocery store, where she
had chosen recently to expose her eyes—and their wariness—their
willingness, now, to assess and retract—a process she would allow
the men to see as it occurred, and though she despised this—there
was the recognition that her prior openness had limits—she saw, at
the same time, their fascination, realized this as a part of the allure of
women who had always seemed somehow "older" than she would ever
be, more "knowing," even when they were young. It was an animal
look—the look of someone interested in survival primarily—that she
hadn't imagined, especially in moments of dismissal, could attract.
But in those moments on the cold glass, her skin seemed even more
pale and translucent—like something not meant to survive, impossible
as protective cover—and the gaze of assessment was trained on her
own face while her body—sinuous and arduously long, angular as a
spider—lay in its mass of hair: puzzling, unforgettable.

29

But there was another subject.

What was it?

It had been deserted by form—

by forms of all kinds.

One could say "river" or "bird" or "fish"

or even "ash"—

and it was none.

And had been none.

And so it was with some irony that this could be

said/felt/thought

on a day that was "beautiful," if cold.

That rivery strands of water fell into a round, raised cement pool

like a river peeing—peeing from eight angles at once.

That a slim tree, the color of ash, was budding

as light hit the ash-grey deck through the greenery

gathered like flowing swords—gathered into

the vase of the earth/the face of the earth

with its many mouths.

Light hit the prayer flags like wind

or wind hit them like light.

But there were no fish.

No birds.

(And the man in the dream said,

You'll just have to feel it

like it is.)

Woman Chained to Fire

As if a field of corn is red and orange in the wind, and she raises her
hand to answer a question; then her other hand. Her bare arms still
suspended above the stalks, the cold metal of the cuffs against her
wrists, as the leaves flap about her thighs, tassels exploding in sparks
near her ribs, the hard and swollen ears of corn shifting their weight
in the thrashing wind, her chains attached so far beneath the tangle
of roots that even though they hold to nothing but flame, she cannot
move. The field is a distant one, far from any house, and the corn,
swaying in its night wind, is growing. Her face is strangely placid.
Rusty silk, drying into curls, pushes toward her mouth, and the corn
plants, now persimmon, now electrifying blue, flicker into each other
like a field of tall and narrow wings, trying to rise altogether into
the air, brushing against her back, flags, the nearly wet slap of their
touch, the rush, the sting, how does she stand, how does she stand it?
What is the question?

Leaves

The green brocade, the layers, like a wall of spring—Ophelia, leonine in tub—Bizet a drape of echo on the tile—masculine, the roar, perhaps while shaving, head thrown back—Kurt, Michael, Reed—closer, red, the gold, our clothed bodies, cushions of support—Sebastian, Cleopatra, Howard, Tom—a spell of foliage below, huge, engorged, enveloping, no summer—the tux, the tie, the white shirt on the hanger—Richard—hunger for the shot glass, for the blue pinot—the time this designates, its pages—grigio, bells, white smoke, the crowd now visible if thin—the ever absent diminution of the distances—the wall, the chairs, the carpeting—the visible, the newly nameable—in our midst, in our mist—the teal, the burgundy, the bronze, the fade to ochre, umber, flattening of foreground/background/memory/imagination—Bill, the unknown center of the room—echo chamber of the shell, the hollow 'round which hardness curves—not gone alone—the gone concurrent blond events, the time of velvet hand to glove—as if an opera—as if a song—the tuneless mirror, spill of paper, crushed and wretched stems, the dust—winter a fact, as usual, behind the fall—and what comes after night that is not morning.

(i.m., W. M.—Vancouver, 2005)

Grille

As if through glass, through windows, in a café, in the afternoon
or early evening, in June, in June or November, month like a fetish
of gray—a month of water hanging onto itself; until it drizzles,
a month of dulled light—he is seen for a moment, accidentally,
between appointments, in the middle of errands, walking down steps,
the cement steps, say, of an old bank—old enough for granite, for
columns—pulling his keys out of his pocket, or gripping the small
black remote that replaces keys (which you can't hear the sound of,
behind all this glass), and approaching his car, so that for an instant you
see his face unguarded—or as unguarded as you will see it—and you
try to memorize it, but it's too fleeting, so that now only the back of his
head, and maybe the veins in his arms that you memorized before (the
way his fingers go, his shirt)—or the waiter comes, the waiter comes
by and asks if you've decided, the waiter comes by and asks if you've
made up your mind—

but this is the opposite of confession.

4

— as, after Odysseus, her body wanted to be Ophelia

The pistol came with its own music.

An echo slid from her throat:

Liquid, alive beyond common names for color.

How at night she could not swim.

Her song like a line of neon in wavering slices

across the crinoline dark

until the dogs began to bay

and men slipped into the skins of animals

to roll against the mud without the barrier of clothes.

How that bay was a living jewel—the sound, the topaz water—

the water had poured from her

and become alive.

She would wash up on the shore or float,

as white as the lizard who pulls the carriage

in a dream, all soggy finery

and hair and reeds.

Over and over

her body was painted

in darkness,

like a wine of skin.

What was true:

It was up to her to invent

her own music,

as she began to hear it

in the growing stain of sky.

7

Because identity had gone

        And no one was waiting

(There was no garden, no stair,

There was no snow)—

        Someone, for instance,

Would not be able to hear

        Callas whisper

All the familiar objects

        Had been removed

There was the sound of traffic—

        But in the morning of a foreign city

Under the upturned corners

        Of the mouth

What was there

        When the muscles went

Why would no one

        Speak about it

It was not a dilemma

        But a state

Air was moving

        Through the scarves of women

Seen from the bus —

        Through cypress,

                Eucalyptus

People held their clothing on,

           Tightly

It was hard to know

        What to hear

Was a film already empty

        The script had been written

The sound of birds

           Infiltrated me

A huge, swaying texture

           Like Beethoven

Soaring out of the Schönbrunn

        A moving curtain surrounding the windows

In and out of sleep

        Walking silently through trees

31

— Mystery Box

What you cannot see is the black river,
how the horizon merges into sand, the sky goes granular—

and what might have begun as clouds,
hills.

Someone has the idea of an oarsman,
standing on a wooden raft,
ferrying a lounging man

and a shape, ambiguous—

from this angle, it looks like a dead horse
or a folded robe.

And the oar no bigger, really, than a needle,

dips into the idea of black, the water scored
like an old LP.

Someone has taken spring away,
and summer,
and water.

You cannot see the ants as they come at your
bare, bloody feet.

You look up
into the endless sand of sky.
There is no sky.

Girl Standing with Death by the Sea

First, there was rain.
Or the surface was scratched.

It was a long distance from green
to green.

Death was so quiet,
so patient.

Perhaps there had been trees.
Living ones.

Or maybe really just rain.
Or scratches.

It reminded her of standing on top of a hill
and looking down at the city trailing below.

No city, though.

Maybe, in the distance, a sail
or a buoy.

Or a sprinkle of stars, recessed
in that intaglio of green.

And a road, curving along the coastline,
but vacant.

It's so different
from standing on the footbridge

with girlfriends, or cousins,
looking out at the noon lake

or turning around at sunset, removing a hat.
Letting the lake go black.

(In another version, the halo was red—
there was a halo in that version.

It covered her head like a hairband
but she was alone.)

She stands, looking out, until dawn
until the greens are mild

shades of blue, and indigo
is the only place that death might be

—or stone—

nothing but a squiggle,
a puzzle piece.

Stationary, somehow.
In little bursts of wind.

It moves like a wet shadow.
If it moves.

Or now it's dark, her hair is longer,
she carries a tambourine

of yellow roses, and death
is only herself, older, and then much older.

The one in the middle—that self—opens her legs in a V,
naked, clasps her hands behind her head—

but she, the sea-looker-she, looks out at the sea.
Feels them, standing behind her.

She has never seen her own exposure, though she feels it.
When she finally sees it—its strangeness, her own—

well, I tell you, I can't explain why,
but it makes her radiant.

Even when everything goes to woodcut white and black,
she stands on a road

and, behind her, it is not death, but a woman with hair—
herself—and skin. And brows. A woman fully exposed

and her dark-clad companion—night, herself.

Or no—the only color now is the palest blue
of water strafed with cloud

and she stands on the black sand before dawn
in her long pale dress and the frothy, possessed black

waves must be wetting her feet and behind her

a figure approaches—a man?
We see them from behind.

She does not yet hear him.

In her private future red bedchamber,
in her long dark confusion of hair,

there is no shame.

Yes—there's a man
and her three selves

as she stands in ochre fog
looking out to the sea.

Her hair spills back
into cloud into branch

she is almost a ghost
he clutches his heart

or maybe just his pocket
the moon reflects in the shape of a lingam

not a pearl—all the way down the water
it makes the road larger, pale and wide

with light until we see her turn away
from the water

and now the reflection, long as the dark the rising
dark of the trees—

it is before, just before, they touch.
Death sits silently by

in another version.

There are so many versions.

No, she was never alone.

Hey, lover. Hey lover, lover, lover. . .

    —after E.M.

Holaday Mason

Holaday Mason is the author of *The Red Bowl* (2016, Red Hen Press), *Towards the Forest* (2007), and *Dissolve* (2011, New River Press, University of Minnesota), as well as two chapbooks. Her manuscript *The Weaver's Body* was a finalist and won honorable mention for the 2014 Dorset Prize, and her chapbook *Transparency* was a finalist for the Snowbound 2015. *The "She" Series: A Venice Correspondence* (with Sarah Maclay) was published by What Books Press in October 2016. Twice a Pushcart nominee, publications include *Poetry International*, *American Literary Review*, *Pool*, *Smartish Pace*, *Runes*, *Solo*, *The River Styx*, *The Spoon River Review*, and *The Laurel Review*. Co-editor of *Echo 681* and poetry editor of *Mentalshoes.com*, she is also a fine art and informal portrait photographer, and has been a psychotherapist in private practice since 1996.

www.holadaymason.com

Wolves Drawn toward the Sound of Bells

At a minimum there is snow,
smooth as the heel of a woman's hand.

Then the snake trails
of the sleigh, marking a passage.

I wonder, were there stars?
And if any fell.

Or was it one of those dawns
when the clouds of breath

are so stunning and pale
you can't look up into heaven

because the problem of beauty
is too immense, the air growing solid,

as the dew of your lungs is spun
into an iridescent web,

clinging to the light,
so fragile as it disappears;

you must turn back
toward each other, wanting

only to feel the damp fleece near your cheeks,
the familiar hand holding your own.

It is still night after all and all around
the sleigh, the dark ring of the woods.

Reciting the Water

Distracted by so many birds careening around in the rain,
I pull over under a row of thrashing trees.

Packs of sodden crows cluster along the telephone lines,
somber notes at the bottom of a bass clef.

Squares of electric light fall from a home nearby
where a mother sings to a child

who already knows what's coming so cries and cries.

This is the opera– thunder, water.

The damp spice of crushed eucalyptus
reminds me of other highways:

owls blacking the hoops of my headlight,

a girlfriend traveling home for Christmas—
one glance (lipstick, purse, rearview mirror)
then her car splintering a quarter mile of trees.

The burned soot of the fields after harvest.

But memory is mutable. Stop. Lift your eyes.
What exactly do you see?

The image of a woman's house shattering in a puddle,
reflection, distortion, then gone.

The faces of everyone I've ever loved slip into and from me,
impossible as holding onto water.

The child in the house is quiet. The sky is a ship of silver.
The birds grow large as they dry. Soon they'll go.

I might have been anyone.

Power

The mock orange like a rumor

is nothing to the wind.
Under the pepper tree's constantly falling leaves

I am small. Stars wound the nothingness
with shreds of light like memories.

This is a concealed backyard. But
it's never really still.

There's someone else's dog, clock, door, bamboo,

TV, chimes, electricity,
everything so filled with movement all the time.

In the darkness, tassels of wisteria—

violent lavender snow. I recall how,

once on the edge of a Pasadena ravine, I was raped
until *in my mind* I agreed to take him

inside, became another woman,

one who consented and so, for a moment,
changed everything.

The Boy Is the Man I Loved

Hand to mouth, I watch
you listen
as I listen, counting

the bright black hairs
at your neck like ribbons binding

a package, the gift of any situation —
present & past— this passage,

like those bodies of water
to which one
always returns.

Your eyes close,
locking away
the meaning of this room.

They stay shut,
waking that furrow—that stream

beside which new deer
might come to stand,
wary & still.

This is where electricity runs—
the daily undulations, from you to me

before we're crushed, as I often crush
the tiny beads of lavender blooms

between index finger & thumb, soaking,
essentially, that death into my body,

which, disappearing, seems so quiet
near the edge of the now-empty stage.

After all, the skin
is a curtain, something to build
an imaginary country beyond.

Your young hand stays all sound—
And every moment is a stranger, an exit wound.

Paris, day 2

6/10/12

Someone is cooing
a turtle dove of morning through
the walls, bathwater streaming
too & motorcycles in the echoes
of the city as faces
in profile stroll past the wrought iron
scrolls at my window—beyond,
the vase of hot raspberry peonies
lit in the flashes of waking sunlight
falling across the table.
I had not expected sex
or had forgotten my body & it's for sure
a woman's sound, opened as the splayed
wings of an ivory bird
& breathless in the undone silk of human skin.
An hour ago, I watched
a boy with smudged oval taped glasses
stare mouth ajar at the tall-legged saxophone
players in the market. New love burst in him this morning
while the cut flowers wagged in their buckets of early summer.
My heart stopped again & began again, something
pure fuchsia, whipping like a strip of lightning,
& how I will miss this world in my mouth,
like the taste of honey, at the end—
if I could just get it all in, just keep singing with
the indigo dawn, waking forever, while farmers sell red
peppers, cherries, apples, storm, red, red
as the breast of the bird who flew into my room in the night—
before the wind raised its voice—
before the thunder opened me
& white hail covered my bed speaking of the future
whispering, again, again,
most certainly sun, most certainly rain.

Old Music

When you remembered to listen, you searched for a room
with good acoustics: vaulted ceiling—

in the air a woman's sighs,
the swish of orchid organza, the lyric notes of the flesh.

At the end of the street, high waves jump the sea wall.

You go inside.
You're told to play the bass guitar,

lean it back against your ribs like your lost widow,
O then rock her in your arms,

until a stained light wounds
your forehead & your hollowness,

until your fingers stagger, drunken dancers
too luminous to know they're no longer young.

Chords are hesitations of silence. Silence has forgotten
itself. The deep thrum on the strings is your skin.

The tango is complicated by our differences.
Play. Dance across the broken black, the white tiles, blazing…

But it is always (I place one white camellia behind each ear)
too quick to have been real—

the subtle cradle of hip in hip, the weeping silk slip
as it hits the floor—this coal in the limbs is a Judas—

a bitter smoke curls.
You ask me for water. I give you rum, say

unzip me slowly. The spine will instruct the mouth.
The mouth speaks of salt & the dead.

I am ruined.
I am ruined— *play*

As Satie Winds Up the Stairs

Someone could not stop

      laughing—

You hovered before & hovered before,
your tongue my leash and then—

      terroir.

The most dangerous act—
the mouth, perch of the soul.

      Over a year
      since

      I'd been kissed.

32

I took you inside.
I took the vein & apple.
I took your stem & held & held.
I took the after & before.
I could not help it.

Bird in storm. Bird under cloud.
Bird.

And inside my cunt, these things arrived:
A bowl of sweet purple blood:
Ten thousand oaks.
Too many moons & pavilions to count.
White sand sifting from my womb like sugar—
your murdered father,
the blue rings on his neck,
on my own,
the lands of grass & those,
those tall standing stones,
huge as men who can see the
black lake so fragile it's invisible
as air & yet it's tumbling with birds,
who sing the
dream where you tell me
I'm not too old.
That it doesn't matter.
It's not too late (did you *speak*?)
This land has no law.

31

Twisting, we smell of wet horses/salt/granite,

(like Christ), in the deep cup of winter
my body is the bridge.

I understand by making circles
against you in the darkness
with my white hips, & see too

all those thousands
of migrating monarchs in Santa Cruz
falling through the eucalyptus grove air/

falling in orange love to death/

(I have known you always
is what the woman says with her body

& knows
& the man knows or
has forgotten or tries to forget)

again, again,

the hundred or more butterflies,
breathless, in pairs
of black skeletal wings,

falling and still with love.

Midpoint Mercury Retrograde

Undone like a whip—my body.
A gnat caught in my palm flutters
& in the morning, a stunned moth on the long table,
wings disappearing into the grain.
Everything is made in the house
of hours—minutes, essence & yes,
my beloved may even lie down in the arms of a lover,
but each kiss is mine, is hers, is ours, revolving in
the black iris of love. The body is the tale of a dash of salt.
Look at me—the heat in my mouth is the sun—is
whole as the soft drum on the soil of ripe plums falling from
the trees, boom, boom. Once after planes drew
hexagrams over the city,
a black crow died on my porch step. It was dawn
on a Sunday, & I, just waking,
in the threads of lights, was *this woman*—
& yes, everything is made & unmade
in the land of our bones, so open me slowly & we
become the velveteen moth—
purple Luna, skunk with damp mineral sugar—
the story of the hidden letters in
the moon void, where I am—
forever lightning.

That Jacaranda, Ten Years Old this August

Insane drip of fanned lace, of green, of splayed,
sprayed droplets flourished easy, of open into,
of the path of music or, as music *in* & through
such thin bright, such flashed open, flirted closed,
collected, fluttered, embarked as froth of thrust
of dapple, as daring calligraphy ever blown like glass
or silk, yes, silken & slithered, & wonder or rather,
—tickle or both—pirouetted in thoughtless grace,
gesture of oboe, cello, scribing, singing the slight
pearly gates, careless caress, precise small sigh
of the of, the always, shimmered chartreuse, drunk,
pure ruffle, waving, calling, crooned, flirted as if the vault
of time is always remembered as "a laughing matter,"
the cure, the signature drawn by tree & sky, folded,
unfolding between tree & sky breathing, breathing
breath of infinity, in its circling lair of making.

Inside the Radio

are these steps I take across this street, some
old movie popcorn, four fresh clams, an empty martini
glass, Miles Davis, twelve white Gerber daisies, a twisted
oak tree, a door, a hallway, an unpacked suitcase
and some golden
bamboo. Inside the radio is
the scent of night blooming jasmine in full bloom. Inside the radio
are many sets of dentures, the electrical currents
that make an epileptic seize, a woman's alto lullaby
sung into her baby's open mouth and a once fine Persian rug.
Inside the radio is the conversation between
two Iranian women walking an Israeli beach
and a bird house full of yellow and green canaries. Inside
the radio are the wheels of a small girl's
roller skates and her furry pink bedroom slippers.
Inside the radio is the sound of falling water.
Inside the radio are eight perfect smoke rings.
Inside the radio are all the old Easter rabbits, a stack of wet firewood,
a newspaper headline from May, 14, 1923 and the two hours
you're allowed to park on the right side of the street in front of your house.
Inside the radio are a bunch of plastic bags
for the dog shit of strange dogs. Inside the radio
is a mother's hand in her mother's hand, is the dew
of Irish wool on a pair of knitting needles,
an orange traffic cone, a lower case letter " l"
and one flawless cherry blossom, open and wet.
Inside the radio is a pair of sandals.
Inside the radio is the twitch of a tail,
three freshly ironed cotton dresses worn by slave women,
a moving violation for jaywalking,
two gangsters, 12 and 11 years old, respectively,
guns in their big pants, carbon on their fingers.
Inside the radio is a watch on a fob,
spinning around, vagrant drumbeats spinning

through the air, the footsteps of a man in your past
(your father? your brother?), the bones of your face,
a pearl of semen on the tip of a penis and
the way an adolescent girl smells of toast and skin.
Inside the radio is some hot Cuban music.
Inside the radio is the Buddha
and his two dogs. Are ten worn out bibles,
and a perfumed soap on a rope.
Inside the radio there are lots of skeletons,
two are in black tie attire. One wears a redressed red dress.
There's the aforementioned music, a wicked chocolate birthday cake,
and the faces of all your relatives carved into masks
you can show to those who are not yet born.
Inside the radio are two roan horses
(the ones you always wanted),
leather saddles, bridles, stirrups
and the fields, the wild new snow fields,
over which to run.

1

The book is still, is closed, so

casts a square shade on the woman's knee
where she kneels at the pond, & still the sorting goes

on—

The book is open, is a question about waiting—

the kiss planted,
want now saturated with a pale cool sheen.

Not knowing any longer—what's behind, what's before,

the woman above & the one below, both
lean & touch mouth to mouth, intently considering

The Face

in the still clear surface, while way up & beyond, vapors of clouds

shape her

hair into white tufting Antoinette coils, the head, a head in clouds
& not in the blood or in the garbage, in the blood or the want.

The pages flutter open.
There is a body lying still.

The body is the mother, my mother.
I spread open her ribs &
count them gently

until they lute & harp / violet glands now fruits & veins steaming
with tenderness. Your mother's here too.

Men will come with boats soon.

It was just a book.
It was a painting in a museum of a woman with a book.

There was a shimmering pool & a world.

Portrait of Child with Mask

*(Transiting Mars conjoins transiting
Uranus in the 4th house before the full moon, 013)*

Dream world, I address you.

Whatever they say, the dark side
of the moon is lit as if one sails to the end

of all & then continues on.

Counsel of yellow rose bush, as a child
I preferred your shade to hot sun,

glued shiny thorns with spit
to my cheeks, my brow, covered my face & arms,

became animal—the thorned beast,

makeshift keeper of the keys
to a sky which otherwise might fall

& break me into many pieces—

what my body knew of space, small boat

freckled, translucent as if made of tissue paper.

No one ever found me hidden in the shadows

of that bush, smelling of roses, smelling of dirt.
A canopy of emerald is a veil of hope.

& now, as the world unravels me

beyond the middle, I ask
what have you been clinging to, little fire?

King of sky, you have my name & have told me
who we become when we remember forever.

The pure side of desire, lost, perhaps knows us
each as simple water falling,
perhaps as one rose or a paper boat

bright with candles sailing silent on a lake
of ink, a lavender dawn, lavender-blue.

Jim Natal

Jim Natal is the Pushcart Prize-nominated author of *52 Views: The Haibun Variations*, *Memory and Rain*, and two previous poetry collections. He also has published three chapbooks and two limited-edition chapbooks. His work has appeared in many journals and anthologies, including *Hayden's Ferry Review*, *Spillway*, *Alligator Juniper*, *San Pedro River Review*, *Beyond Forgetting: Poetry and Prose About Alzheimer's Disease*, and *New Poets of the American West*.

A former NFL creative executive, he directs The Literary Southwest series at Yavapai College and is the publisher and co-founder of Conflux Press.

Windchime Tantra

Everything we can do with our bodies
already has been done,
patterns of hands or legs described, given names
in ancient texts, little poems with mouths and eyes:
standing cranes,
the grape cluster,
dragonflies.

I know your body so well,
quirks and contours of your skin,
like the tall boy who looks out across familiar
shaded waves of hills, grass prairies
in the wind with one lone tree,
eyelids half-closed sees
a figure that beckons
with finger bent, smooth kestrel beak,
persistent and light as windchimes in the night,
perhaps it's you.
And he knows it is time to leave home,
emerge a man from your embrace,
marry animal and tame,
to sweat in the night
then to sleep
seamless against the backs of your thighs
until body heat throws off the covers
and bedroom breeze brings relief.

River eels,
emperor's delight,
blossoming branches intertwined...

I could map your body, and in my mind
I do
when cold and early I'm alone,

a jetstream away in some hotel room
unable to remember my dreams,
and snow is coming down,
trucks picking their way on drifted
dark interstates.
I think of ranchers and their sons
rising intent on chores with
icy pails,
orbs of brown cow eyes, thick tongues,
steaming, lowing beasts inside a slatted wooden barn,
the only light ablaze for miles.

I think of pleasure when I'm awake beside
your scent,
the length of you taking my measure:
mantis,
floating lotus,
birdwings,
garden of sighs.

Held notes of windchimes fade on distant porches.
I sleep again, curled in the den of your breathing.

What They Do

Me cortaron la voz / dos voces tengo.
They cut out my voice / I have two voices.
—Alicia Partnoy

This is what they do when you disagree,

when you cast your vote in a well that has no bucket, when
the rope has been used for other purposes,

when you live for years under house arrest and the house
is your mother's, when there are no charges against you
but electric,

when interrogation is philosophy, when prison is a commandeered
schoolhouse—you are locked either
in or out,

when police protection takes on
a more subtle meaning, when poems are
verdicts,

when you pour out your wine to fill the bottles
with gasoline, when even your blood is flammable, when your blood
is dammed,

when your friends and their wives hide their wrists, when
the children are candles,

when sleep becomes a memory and memory sleeps, when concrete
and wire are comforting, when all colors are shades of
steel and tin,

when maps are folded into smaller and smaller squares, when
doors stay closed and windows become exits, when curtains are
black leather,

when all the birds molt into sparrows and you feed them
crumbs of metal, when leaves are stapled onto branches now
there will never be a fall,

when the light goes out and there is no difference.

This is what they do when they fear your other voice more
than anything they have taken or lost, more than beating
clocks, dripping spigots, and tiny whirring insects
in the silence of their night.

Rest Area

Forest fires raged in Idaho that summer
when you pulled off the Interstate

east of Boise, parked, and cut the engine.
Your whole body vibrated with

the churn of tires, slipstream of distance
spreading like a concrete wake behind you.

The air was thick with char; sky
smoke-damaged the orange-gray

of an August steel town dusk.
You held the wheel, didn't you,

as if afraid to let go, watched plumes
rising over ridges of evergreen hills,

turned the music off. A car door unlocked
beside you. A woman stood, wary, pistol

holstered on her belt, infant strapped
to the front seat, belongings piled in back.

You were faceless, weren't you, simply part
of her scan. You walked behind the buildings

for a better view of the fire; when you
returned to your truck, she was gone.

You can drive for days in
this country, for static-filled

nights on end, plotting the points
on a graph of your restlessness—

Albuquerque, Salt Lake, Reno, Yuma,
Bakersfield, Spokane, Laramie, Lincoln—

assembly line of interchangeable destinations,
miles strung between like troughs of wires.

Sometimes people stop on these highways,
never get back on, hole up, flickering,

in disappeared motels to wait it out,
adopt a mutt and a *TV Guide*,

hotplate dinners and beer cans. Not you.
Because you think you will just keep

driving, follow taillights as if Polaris,
your life held to the right of parallel

yellow lines (divided, then broken),
a bird that cannot sleep, its instinct

only for migration, pausing
to feed and briefly rest.

When there's no arrival,
what can leaving mean?

Somewhere the mountains are being
consumed; ash is drifting like souls.

Rain in L.A.

Saturday sunset

Lorca writes: "They do not think
of the rain and they've fallen asleep
suddenly as if they were trees." I don't
think of the rain either. It *isn't* raining.
Somerset Maugham never wrote "Rain."
I think I'll go to the carwash.
There is no such thing as rain or evolution.
No drizzle, spatter, drip, or seep.
No water stains. No swishing branches,
brushes on cymbals riffing
in river-cryin' jazz lounge time.
We don't need no stinking umbrellas,
no newspapers folded into sinking
upturned boats, inky runnels of hard
luck stories streaming down faces
and the backs of necks. I refuse
to believe in the afterlife of rain,
in drowned angels or Lucifers, no bibles
crumbling like soggy matchbooks.
There is no poetry in the rain,
no reason to bother thinking up
even 17 syllables about it. I hear
no music in the rain on a tin roof,
no rodent scuttling, fingertapping,
teeth clacking, hammer pounding,
machine gunning steel band calypso
against the windows. I do the limbo
under the rain. I fly below the radar
of the rain. I laugh in the face of you, Rain.
I'm wearing rain-patterned camouflage;
the rain falls right by me, can't see me.
And what if it could?
I've become the rain, made a friend
of rain, am one with the rain. It rains,
therefore I am.

Borderline

Mexico is bleeding people.
I am opening the sky for them.
Some smell of ochre earth.
Some are calloused as paws.
Others just refract light.
A few speak only in breezes.
I can taste the fires
in the kitchens they left behind.
Their cold matches
rattle like dried insects in my mouth.

Martín crossed near Patagonia, Arizona.
I did not open the sky for him.
Instead, I parted the river.
I walk along its banks waiting
for ocotillo to bloom; the manzanita
has such red branches…even now.
Only a *pendejo* or a *bruja* can see
beyond the chain link and flowers
with petals so large
they hide us from *la migra*.

You know what they always say:
"*El viento sobre la tierra tumba muertos.*"
Ah, yes, this land's remorseless wind
does blow away the dead.
Sunshine spills melancholy
as Martín collects rattlesnakes
and puts them in his pockets.
Puma won't sit beside him
when they stop for water—
he will stand only, tell his stories
from a distance, speak of neon cities
in some future north where it will rain
sticky money on them all.

Their haggard map points the way
to intersections with no corners.
But that's the way it is
once you pass *la linea.*
The gash is 2,000 miles long
and all the barbed wire in the world
cannot suture the wound.

Lost. One-footed Adult Crow. Reward.

Maybe it should have said: "FREE" instead of "LOST."
Maybe it's the same crow I hear down the block
puncturing the morning with insistent counterpoint
to the soap-smooth Sunday dove songs.
And "LOST" to whom? One creature's lost
is another's escape. But now that it's back
among the power lines and madronas, this crow
really could be adrift, homeless and dressed
in shabby black, roosting in doorways
wrapped in atrophied wings.

There's the obvious question of how the crow lost
its foot, what led to its pet name of Hopalong, Long John,
or, perhaps, Lefty. Did it happen when it was young or grown?
Or was it born that way, its whole life a balancing act?
Crows are so smart. Curiosity or boredom
could have gotten the better of it. And with sharp-edged
suddenness, the idea of spending its maturity in someone's care
became more necessary than ludicrous: kind words,
a guaranteed ear, the certainty of scheduled meals,
a place to sleep with both eyes closed.

And about that reward: If the crow is returned,
accepts again its cage and perch or even comes back
on its own to reclaim its low-ceilinged kingdom,
will it be win-win all around? The owner regains
a live-in jester. The crow can relax, take a load off its foot.
And the alert-hearted Samaritan, who at first
refused the crisp twenty, now slips it in
with the other bills on the way down the back stairs.
It's almost like one of those Asian teaching tales—
how the unfortunate open window leads in as well as out.

Photographic Memory

II

After the second fireball had singed us all
and the world turned into a negative,
after the images had been replayed, replayed,
and replayed until we could replay them
at unwilling will, and after the ash had elbowed
through the streets and the flurries of business
paper had drifted and the face of the devil
had been traced in the smoke and the leaping bodies
had embraced gravity one final time
and were not orderly in their fall like bowler-hatted
Magritte men and were not surreal but all too real,
and the gray tentacles had engulfed the buildings
and pulled until they collapsed, and after
the smoldering and the compressed eternity
of digging, dismantling, and disposal,
when hope had been sifted and sorted,
and there were not hands to go with fingers
wearing rings set with stones born and returned
to the heat and pressure, after the tattered flags
and the incessant nights of seeing and coughing,
vigils beside posters grieving on chain link fences,
the photographs from desks and wallets and walls
were found and restored, were survivors
in place of survivors.

In Memory of Her Memory

IV

The horse that is my mother's memory
has run away. It hasn't gone far;
we can see it standing on the hill beside
our property, a silhouette at twilight.
I don't know who feeds or curries it now,
or if it has gone completely feral.
Sometimes the horse will come close, stand
just out of rope's reach. She calls to it,
then whispers of their past together.
The horse nickers and snorts softly
when she mentions Philadelphia or Chicago.
Its long neck extends and the horse shakes
its head when she talks about my father,
how she misses him, how people still
stop her on the street or in the grocery store
to tell her they miss him, too.
The horse doesn't seem to mind
that she repeats herself so often. No one
recalls when the horse got out
or who left the stable door open,
but perhaps the horse will return on its own
and we'll find it early one morning in its stall
munching hay and burnished oats.
We'll stroke the velvet blaze on its forehead,
reach into our back pockets
for those special carrots it loves.
And, if we're lucky, the horse
will linger for a while, maybe
lead us to the place where it last saw
my mother's missing hearing,
which also slipped away silently
while we were all asleep.

Underwater. As if there's been a catastrophic flood. As if we're
living in the backfill aftermath of the construction of a massive dam,
watching appraised values submerge like towns. We're so deep now we
need scuba tanks to view the sunken ruins. At least I've got a roof over
my head. My father, who went through the Great Depression, would say
something like that. Now I've got a house and a depression of my own.
And a roof over my head that leaks when the snowmelt begins. We put
pinging pots out to catch the drips like Ma and Pa Kettle. Be thankful
you've got a pot to piss in, my father whispers. He's far beyond this.
Dad, you can put all the béarnaise sauce you want on a shit sandwich.
It's still a shit sandwich.

Oh, Evanescence!
I wrote you a lovely song
except now it's gone.

My student writes about his last day in Iraq, the one that ends with his getting blown up by an IED. I try to separate form from content the way the insurgent separated my student from much of his blood and nearly his life. His essay needs a lot of work—spelling, punctuation, flow. *Point and support, point and support* I drone to the class. No argument without example. No blast without detonation.

The rules of grammar,
dispassionate as a bomb;
each wire connected.

After Paris in December I walked the beach. Los Angeles never looked
so Gaugin, the city of sunshine as opposed to the City of Light so "old
and cold and settled in its ways." The high clouds had been washed
with white ink on blue, fat *sumi-e* brush strokes breaking up as they
tailed off to the East, the mountains and then the desert. The tide
was far receded, revealing an avenue of wet sand that mirrored the
sky and made walking an act of levitation. It was late afternoon and
a few people had begun to gather, staking out their spaces to watch
the setting of the winter sun. Almost all were alone and had settled
equidistant from each other exactly like the gulls standing at the surf
line facing out to sea. In a moment of shared reflection, even the ocean
withdraws into itself.

No clump of seaweed—
twisted neck, feathers, web feet:
a dead cormorant.

The dead cormorant
trussed in fishing line, hooks set,
flying to new depths.

Jesus, St. Anthony, St. Simeon on His Pillar

One desert thornbush pretty much resembles another,
burning or not. The sightline sameness of ridges on the
magma horizon. Washes appear as trails, spaces
between pink boulder piles, between sun-sucking,
water-hoarding plants each seem to lead to apparitions.
You can wander endlessly, aimlessly, as if lost in
datura-induced visions and prayers—*Oh, lead me not
into temptation, into winding petroglyph canyons*—
neglecting to leave enough daylight for the return journey.
Suppose you have to spend the night, another and another
until all that mattered doesn't matter anymore. A closetful
of clothes, some still with tags; cabinets of dishes,
pots and pans; small electric appliances; pantry stocked;
a fast car left locked in a gravel highway pullout; cell phone
useless as on the darkest side of the moon. Good riddance,
you think. No, you say it aloud. But only the red-eyed
Phainopepla on the Joshua Tree spike, the Cactus Wrens
in mid-mating ruffle, can hear what the devil wind doesn't
devour, disseminating like the birds the seeds of the self.

Gratitude
(The Gospel According to Arnie's Accountant)

"I'm thankful for the things I have and all the things I don't."
—Chris Knight, "Enough Rope"

I know enough to know I don't know enough.
And I know enough to be grateful.

So many reminders of what can go wrong and does,
so many wheels within wheels turning, grinding.

DNA daisy chains twist, the luck of the draw and
the draw of luck. Go home, be happy you've got one.

Say thanks at every opportunity; you don't have
to wait for the turkey to be set upon the table.

It's even less than brief, a blur then gone. Be cautious
or be bold but no matter how hard you try there's always

a split-second of inattention: the campfire spark that
drifts away, the dropped knife caught by the blade.

It's reflex, it's reaction. It's natural. Hoard or share,
accept or deny. You can make it. You can spend it.

But you can't keep it.

Jan Wesley

Jan Wesley's first book of poetry, *Living in Freefall*, was published in 2007. She has three published chapbooks, and her poems have appeared in the *Iowa Review*, *Rattle*, *Pool*, *Spillway*, *Solo*, *Yalobusha Review,* and *Psychological Perspectives*. She received a Pushcart nomination and was a Ruth Lily award nominee. She received her MFA at Vermont College, and taught Creative Writing at University of Redlands, and various writing courses at The Fashion Institute of Design and Merchandizing in Los Angeles. She works now as a freelance writer, editor, researcher, and teaches private writing workshops in Los Angeles.

The Problem with the Mail

I write to a man and address it
to so-and-so in Idaho.

He steps outside, brings an axe down
on an erupted root, splits the earth in two
with the flat side of his knees
as he sinks into a stretch of road
that meanders towards Canada.

I want to know the women he finds
pet names for, which ones press on
his abdomen, work him into sand.

I want to fluff up the hair of his linings,
walk past him under a barrel of clouds,
drag a toe, lead with an elbow to stretch

and mock him with soft skin that lies
in the cavern beneath the tongue.

He curls under the blade of a shadow
to smoke a little before he trudges home
to slide around on rubber casters
of his desk chair in front of a glass wall
that slams into the west face of the Rockies.

He slips on a pair of tinted glasses
to read my letter, feel my breath stand
on its own by his slowly reclining body

as I beg him to give me a new mouth, stuff
me like fowl, teach me to say anything.

Double Exposure

"If your pictures aren't good enough,
you're not close enough."
— Robert Capa

The Nikon is carried the way Mother
taught me, strap around neck, hand
cupped under the lens, ready to pull
the viewfinder up for that sudden instant
a child leaps from the peak of a swing
or a bullet leaves the barrel of a gun.
She taught me to trap the tragic
circumstance as a woman high
on adrenaline lifts a car off her son
or a girl poached in poverty looks
at the camera, her predator, the shooter
anticipating what comes at the end
of the click. Mother owned photographs
like Capa's soldier captured as he's shot,
feet dug into the earth he's stumbling
from, body in a crescent, arms flung
like wings, more the way a skydiver
falls face to earth than a man dying.
I shoot for sport today, ten rolls lumped
in my pocket like coal. A boy no older
than I was when Mother died drags
his feet in an effort to walk with dignity
and if the light was right, I'd ask to take
his photo from the chest up, deteriorating
legs out of view. A woman loops her arm
through his, turning sideways to listen,
laughing deeply from damaged lungs
the way my mother would, black hair
pinged by blasts of sun, weight on toes
of her shoes as she'd bend over frosted
glass of the boxy Rolliflex, eyes scanning
the target, index finger cocked and waiting
at the button, coaxing human frailty to her,
whispering *come on, comeon, comeon, comeon….*

Working the Weekend

First is your long calved leg as it finds a way
from under padded cover, and a peek of hair

flits through the muzzled light, my fingers
working like a wound to seek tenderness

and comfort. I forget how journeys back
to work remind me of days away, chasing the past

in Monterey Bay in 1997, feeding fish to seals
with your children, and the useless shade of palms.

Your other leg drops away from the bed, my face
in tired wakefulness for you as I touch

your skin, its golden hues from ranch sun,
a neighbor's motor bike slipping gears as it sails

into hilly dry horizons. The malady of morning
news is lifted from asphalt and we could never live

in this silence, every stumble from davenport
to the bed pawing at the pelvis and both of us

grazing each other with our hands for balance.
Birds at the window mock their own song as you

ask which freeway I take, crawling up and off
your confident abdomen until soon we notice

how seeds of the living have bloomed overnight
and ashamed we argued until dawn, how visible

to wrath we feel now so we leave it at that. You
flick away pages of a slept-upon story and we kiss

before I drive with the movie in my trunk to a home
of executives who furrow in Malibu to find love,

to tell me what they expect next, something daring,
like man meets woman, stranger kills everybody.

My Old Man Gets Sick and Dies
and Leaves this Hole in the Universe

1.

He still drives around
the neighborhood, voice the texture
of hammered rocks, humming to KJAZ. Crazy

how a car might pull up to a light, a ridge of grey
hair lying low along an unkempt collar,
copycat image making me

double-take, double-take,

but it's not him. And it's not
the guy walking at dirigible pace, black
beret cocked to one side as he watches closely

for that nick in the sidewalk that might send him
flying. And it's not the guy at the counter
rubbing a ten-dollar bill

with a scratchy crackle
making certain a fiver isn't attached
to it. I feel the pain of his death for an eternity, not

excessive considering 15 years in Pennsylvania, then
35 of that breezy California lifestyle where
I labored through years of lost

concentration, ingesting
an impressive index of chemicals, stunned
and carefree like dad on morphine before the body stopped.

2.

After the quiet I feel the box of his Pacemaker, slip off
his watch, wriggle the bent finger till it's free
of its gold band, my hands

cupping his freezing face.
Imperceptible like time moving (or not)
my arms go to where a rib is still cracked, the final unhealing

bone, and no matter how long I sit, ear to his chest, there is
no heft of air in or out as his skin loses tension, no
worries anymore, 3:40 pm, December 14th.

3.

Last night's sleep was kinder
than ether, dulling a trepidation I might not lose
sight of that final dropped guard of his dignity – weakened knees,

spine grouted with pain – insistent as I was for him to take pill
after pill *for the pain, dad*, since he couldn't quite
think of them as a miracle. I am selfish,

unprepared for him to disappear,
our daily rants ripped away like sheet from person
needing to be identified, and I'd give him carte blanche to pound

more sense into my ailing lack of it if only he could've stuck
around. By January I visit the city he grew up
in, New York's light

invasive as I walk around
the biggest hole in the earth, so deep & depressed
I balance my weight on a crate at the end of a taped-off street

gazing down at metal cranes and tangled cement to see what
will replace the Towers – the twisted rebar and ghostly
ash – until security tells me to move.

4.

I figure I'll polish off
that image of his trembling hands
and teeth the morning he died, so I drink at the Algonquin,

with priceless rugs, plush seats, every marble table surrounded
by suited business pros propped up by privilege.
My father coveted none of the above

but liked photos plastered edge
to edge along the walls above his desk – the ones
of sisters and brides and cousins and Einstein and V.I. Lenin

who led a revolution the year my father was born. Three months
from now I imagine my mother will have to
take the photos down and we will drive

around the neighborhood
hearing shopkeepers take note of his absence,
asking after him as people do from porches where dad sipped

vodka, wanting to be like any other guy you never see until
he's gone, the lack of him tumbling off the stoop
and into your unsuspecting lap.

First Boy

Just imagine. The first beautiful boy I ever knew
was a slender strawberry blonde, paleness

peppered in brown freckles, skin and hair
singed with salmon red. The blue in his eyes

ran all the way to the back of his head

and how those eyes must have shone
amazement as planes lifted up and over

unfamiliar breadth of water, jagged
outlines of Pyrenees, sluggish transport

guzzling oil by the Red Sea, swooping past
Himalayas, Bay of Bengal, nosing towards

rice paddies, ancient Buddhist temples,
those mispronounceable landscapes

at the farthest end of the world. Poolside, on
patches of lawn, we liked to watch him lift barbells

made in the factory downtown, and imagine
how we felt as the black iron hit his chest, then

dipped back to the cement, sometimes 50 times
before someone's mother picked us up at five.

Knowing that young girls could ruin him,
he'd say bah-bye, sunburned neck inclined to one

side, maybe to have a closer look. And just
imagine the look he had as he was hit and spit

smoke-high into the air, that first boy I ever knew
to die in Vietnam, his fear-scorched skin opening

beyond what one should ever be allowed to feel.

After Midnight

We're gonna stimulate some action;
We're gonna get some satisfaction.
We're gonna find out what it's all about.
After midnight, we're gonna let it all hang down.
        — JJ Cale / Eric Clapton

In the days before drought we threw
umbrellas in the trunk and the men washed
their cars regardless of moody skies, slippery
bands of clouds scuttling along the horizon
daring us to scamper in heels & sleeveless
to the clubs, where women strutted hiked-up
skirts and flirty ways we'd flip our hair, show
our teeth with please and the boys would
follow us in to Outlaw Blues & smoky clubs
along the strip where stripping was not the main
event but music music music was a nightly
draw, cruising like topless Corvettes to find
Who We Would See that night, who was Hot
& who was going to plummet from the stage
into waves of arms, who could play the longest
solo, who might bring a friend who'd opened
for Janis, how the stairs would curl around
to the ladies room loaded with "Boo" & gossip
and who would have a little something extra
like white powder or Leary on a postage stamp
& we'd swoon to the beat of anyone playing
live & bare-chested or swooping a bottle
of Jack from the trembling floor, music mid-
week at the Central with cheapest drinks in town
and bands playing like Jimi on the way up
up up & lady-frontmen singing it sultry & loose
like life depended on a 1st beat of a bass drum
& we danced and we whirled and Thursdays
out-of-towners played the Lingerie, staying

open later than Gazarri's, three floors sizzling
along Sunset, and if we were lucky a semi-stud
celebrity would take us into On The Rox, drunk
as truckers or thieves, girls rubbing up to guys
in cowhide & skintight jeans, silky shirts undone
to the bones staying hard, hard, the guiiii-tars
slashing the skin, our feet weeping as we'd slam
into the dark, following strangers & sweeping
the long boulevard for cops, kisses that could last
into a lavender and threatening dawn, stroking
the skin with temptation & a lather of attention,
stumbling into 3 a.m. silence, our ears ringing
with promises to see each other *later, baby*,
later & I'll see you again, two, three, four, one…

Stroll

Sunday morning is a kind of church
of its own, cars easy-going and parked
in grazing formation along the curb
in front of the real church with invitation

to just about everyone, damp air
relieving stress and devotion, sleek
bodies strolling the reservoir. A neighbor
with a hybrid dog passes by, his saunter

tinged with performance, assurance
of a pleasant day of rest, the 7th day
when beach kids liked to say that *god
went surfing.* Mushy and sentimental

I let the mind saunter on and take in
smells, the way dogs drag those noses,
straining at their rope's end for silent
treats. I stumble a bit on cement cracks

and find a loose stone to kick, remember
dancing the can-can, skirt thrown
and taffeta shaken in front of my face,
tossing glances like coins and wishing,

wishing for life to begin. I hang sharply
to the right around a chartreuse junction
of the iron fence, as if my toes are tiny
insect legs changing direction, the red

graffitied stop sign holding back cars,
my gaze moving along telephone poles
losing themselves in beautiful vertical
lines, a graphic creation of what rises

toward sky, tickling the eye and memory.
I pass pedestrians and rotate my head
on a healing neck, utter salutation
and there is sadness as people barely look

at me, another species unable to push
against the grain, to lie down in the grass
as I do, like spreading out on tucked sheets
and mauling old lovers with my freedom.

Duets for the End of Time

1: August, 2000

The Atlantic is maniacal with white caps.
We pilot through rubberized seaweed & fast

food cups, the jumbo size, a hive of children
on the shore. Naively, I want you to like this

press of flesh into galaxies of sand, the rise
of the tide, its slavish nature toward *la luna*.

We leave footprints in an anarchistic toss
like flung clothes, like your ancestors spread

from porches in Nashville to Harney Peak.
The rocks have taught you everything

about stability and subterranean movement.
Our lives happen like typewriter keys, *whop*,

like a bash of waves climbing the sand, inching
toward our blanket, our shoes, the miniature

bar in the basket. You take off like a sprinter
as our daughter stands up to the first wave

and rushes into the ocean, and another
wave lifts her to the other side into spinning

water and I look where there is her usual fish-like
undulation, the usual arc of her arm over shoulder,

hand spiking like a spade when I see her
disappearing, every pop of her mouth out for air

gasping harder. My chest tightens as you hit
the water and dive and soon the idea of family

seems yanked away like bodies through an open
door of a plane, no sound comparable to screams

from panicked tones you don't know are yours,
no speed to match the *whoosh* and the pounding

of water as you try to save Anna from being
dragged to sea, every physically operating bone

in her driving toward land, slides clicking
behind her eyes of what she's done with

her life or, as she'd say it, what she *hasn't* done,
and you make that last set of curls, her

mouth open, neck arched forever, her body
nothing but a hand that's gripping, then letting go.

2: Thanksgiving, 2001

Nothing but white noise from an altitude
of twenty stories, facing northwest to the Empire

State and the Met Life Tower with its glowing
dome. Blonde hair from the dog peppers black

dress clothes as we step out of patent shoes
and down martinis southeast of the living

room window where a pasty din of perpetual
smoke is gripping the city and still there is

the sifting of piles of jewelry and any nub
to fingerprint, the workers straining unending

debris through fingers of biohazard gloves,
then over and over the dumping of piles

of powdery ash onto Staten Island. You lie
beside me, unzip the dress I wear a year after

Anna's funeral and now the Towers down, too.
Only you know I will die in mourning, years

down a road that grudgingly we will get to.
You leave me for my inevitable drill of sleep

I cannot control, drifting off as a breeze
meanders into our room where, before Anna died,

we'd crumple to the floor, clothes on, madly
kissing the lids of each others' eyes in lieu of true

vision, our heavy petting an incandescent
glow, our features disappearing as they do now

in a shoreline fog that just by its nature is so
uncaring of what it takes and will never give back.

3: July, 2002

The new neighborhood joint has two-dollar
well drinks and pans simmering with limp food.

I lean across the backless tops of pickled women
to snatch a Stoli off the bar. You chat up

a German with gleaming teeth who's so
young he is soaked in the American dream.

We leave at midnight when I am drunk
and weave our way to a taxi, *clack, clack*

into the side of a Datsun, *ding, ding*, shin first
into the bumper of a limousine, tugging

on the handle of the wrong yellow door, knees
buckling under regret and threat of annihilation

from determined traffic. Life is a cat's cradle
of whispered innuendoes, but we are

boisterous all the way to Amsterdam and 83rd.
You sleep in a chair, feet wrapped in weeds

on the roof garden, and there is a miracle of bells
tolling to warn us that things still aren't right.

4: August, 2003

I exhale smoke in a steady stream, my plug
pulled, the stifling heat pinning me to sheets

damp and syrupy. You arrive late with roses
and complaints. Unending alarm and news

from the war lure me to the brink of dumbness.
There is separation of consonants from words,

vase from snap dragons and I want to see
cattle outside Au Sable Forks, but severe

storms are reported on the weather channel.
Numbers have risen to a half a million

soldiers gone to the Mid-East and tomorrow
we have promised dinner for a couple who lost

their son in Baghdad. Rain begins to clobber
the roof like a drum, lightning striking one

state away across the bridge and even in this
heat I light a row of candles, think about fire

ignited between us, and without words you
make a contented woman out of me, each

of us seeking a hardened nipple, a forgetting
of the ceaseless ache as we try for a new way in.

Brenda Yates

Brenda Yates grew up on military bases. After Tennessee, Delaware, Florida, Michigan, Massachusetts, Japan and Hawaii, she settled first in Boston, then Los Angeles.

Her poems appear in numerous journals and anthologies including *Mississippi Review*, *City of the Big Shoulders: An Anthology of Chicago Poetry* (University of Iowa Press), and *The Southern Poetry Anthology, Volume VI: Tennessee* (Texas Review Press). Awards include a Pushcart nomination, the Beyond Baroque Literary Arts Center Poetry Prize, a Patricia Bibby Prize and honorable mention in the Robinson Jeffers Tor House Poetry Contest. Tebot Bach published her first collection, *Bodily Knowledge*, in 2015.

The Universe's Clock

Sunlight mixed with slow days, shimmered roadside weeds and overgrown fields into fires of their own. Heat settled on my shoulders, soaked my back, loosened my legs making me limp as a daisy-chain necklace. I'd forgotten: the humid simmering of so-hot-you're-dizzy summers before *chilled air*. Dirt in the creases of a boy's sweaty neck, the streaky rivulets. When men took off hats to wipe forehead, temples, neck with folded handkerchiefs. When women dabbed upper lips with hankies bought in boxes. Fine ones, wrapped in tissue paper, with embroidered edges: initials, violets, bluebirds or pale roses like those on the scalloped wrist of a *Missy's* fancy cotton glove. I was remembering the propped-open doors of Main Street merchants, corner drugstores with fountains for cherry cokes, root beer floats and banana splits—then I heard it: *Ssss. Tsk.* As though thousands of flywheels started spinning at once, each one soundless, but all together, moving the air. A hissing, without the anger, and then the click, like a small gear shifting. *Ssss. Tsk.* I kept walking. Pools formed on the blacktop ahead, then moved on, leaving no trace of slick or wet. Softened tar muffled my footsteps. *Sss. Tsk.* That was all. Later, I heard it again, between the stoned grooves of albums I played. It scared me enough to tell the fortuneteller who lived on my floor. She said something about Andrew's marvelous times, wings, backs, chariots, and *hurry on dear* before slamming the door. But she was drunk, so perhaps I misunderstood.

Demarcations

At those latitudes, day went on as if
it would never end. Mostly, I gave in
before it did. But even sticking it out,
I'd somehow miss its surrender
between blinks. Sitting on the back steps
as my mother's voice lost its sharp edges,
I'd angle myself to watch her freckled
hazel irises recede into black. Her pupils
like a night animal's keeping light
as it faded. And me trying to catch darkness
as it happened, before she lit a cigarette.
But I never did. Match flared. I'd wince,
and all around was night.

At these latitudes, shadows extend
themselves. No billow or fade. Afternoon
slants and all its objects—poles, trees, even
houses—stretch across streets, up slopes,
to the edges of night as it awakens.
Bright voices drift, carried on the breeze,
and like the child who doesn't want day
to end, light has not yet let go. There's
maybe a green flash as it jerks and settles,
as the air shifts and turns its face
toward the sky, as I give in to the cold
rush of what she'd called the darkness
grazing us.

Seven Ways of Reckoning

I
At the edge of dusk, sea meets the land and sighs,
murmuring rhythmic wind-lost words
as though crooning;
her dark voice of gathered ends
unfolding night, like a lullaby.

II
We are all the sea, he tells me—water
invented bodies as a way to get
around. I wanted to believe eyes
blue as the darkest ocean, but even
then felt his restless heat. And who can
not love fire? Even air is drawn.
Fire has its ways. As for the rest, wishes
are silky ash or mists of afterthought.

III
After buying stuffed quahogs at the beach-
shack window, we sit on the seawall eating
salty flesh, toss back the shells. Waves slap,
suck at the sand and take them one by one.
Final arbiter, gizzard and maw, unmaking
what she gave birth to. Even sailor
children who glide away in painted boats,
sunfish or catamarans, are but soft bones
anchored to her belly, and the pulse we need
blisters hulls to remind that she, in time,
will take us back, breath by breath.

IV
There's blood on the moon and trees talking
nonsense, and too loud. But if I cover my ears,
it's the sea that calls and sea that answers,
humming beneath the watery luster of my skin.

V

Harbor seal. Its mid-section a gaping hole.
Parenthetical printed on the sand: (shark
attack, single bite, escape) punctuated
with drag marks of hauling ashore. Visible
signs of invisible order as when, tonight,
scavengers that have been smelling death
all day, move down from the hills unless,
unless the tide has already come back.

VI

The cubists had it right, you said, ducking beneath
the boom, the seeing and seeing and seeing.
Wind takes the sail; we hiss away. Boyish lover,
reservoir of lilacs and thorns, owning my cheekbones
with a careless touch. I still dream of your prickly
heart and the sad dances when your body whispered
in my hands, still feel brown shoulders damp
from a night swim, and the wrists I tried to hold,
and how you broke away. I still wake seeing
you run from the car on the bridge at Buzzard's
Bay, and the way you leapt, not into the water,
but onto the rocks—to be sure.

VII

Falling off the edge of myself, I move inland,
grow excessively fond of roses and wild
jonquils, or is it daffodils? I haunt old graveyards,
walking among broken-winged angels who
long since gave up all pretense of anything but
merely holding on to the pitted stones as they
return to dust. But night comes; wind carries
me back to the water, still humming her tuneless
strains, to breathe all that's falling into the sea.

Melancholy Anagrams

Lonely elm
local men—
lean, homely, lame, coy, mean—
a yell: come one,
come all alone

oh meal! oh holy hymn!
yea melon, ham, hen, clam
ah cello, clan hall, yeah
comely loch, lane, lye

§

Hey, lynch man,
heal each ache—
Mac, Ella, Lyle—
cleanly lace each hole on Alec,
Neal, Amy, Len

Hey, he-man,
manly one,
hem each hymen,
lance each cell,
each coal hole

Hey, clay man.
heal one once a Holly,
a Noah, a Honey,
an ocean once a home,
a name, a halcyon
calm only
hell can loan.

Martini II

There's no way to count the endless permutations
of a snowflake and no matter how many words Eskimos
are said to have,
there are myriads hooked to any mouth

as in drifts, as in loose powder, fresh powder,
hard-pack, flurry, squall or slant-fall,
sleety needles or feather-flakes,

driven whether wet or dry,
able to create a frost bath, an ice-crust,
and falling heavy or light,

maybe is ice-fall, like hailstones,
more akin to some tropospheric scatter,
or interference creating static on a screen,

or better yet, the way it hisses and clicks, touching the ground
with its crisp, new-metal smell

or worse, as in snowy, meaning wintry
as an aged one's hair or the beard of one approaching death,

it can mean sprinkled with confectioner's sugar, a drug,
or clean linen white as white can be, as in pure, as in bleached,
it's a kind of bird, a type of wolf, leopard or flower,
patterns of bloom as well as showers of dying blossoms,
tonight: a dusting of snow, tomorrow: blankets of it,

and depended on
for the way it accumulates on mountains,
snowpack, creating the kind of melt that makes a river;

brightly white, as of plumage, fleece or breasts,
thus extending itself to soft and desirable,

or the just opposite—it chafes
as when dendrites send information to the cell body
and axons take information away—call it what it is:

a chemical/electric storm,
and the synapse a chasm
for the blizzard

Another Place I Don't Want to Leave

The island breath of ginger and plumeria
follows us to the harbor mouth, already
a sweet nostalgia. Open sea swallows
orientation and perspective disappears.

Now, only an endless ocean the sky
curves into and a clean wind
scrubbed by miles of nothing.
Schools of flying fish leap past portholes
as if to see eye to eye
this massive something
moving through their midst.

From the upper deck, waves
flatten to ripples of no consequence,
powerless even, or so it seems
when we get our sea legs.

We watch the sky for a sliver of moon,
serene as it rises, for the Milky Way
spilling its river of stars
to the black edges of earth,
for the blaze of sunrise
that erases stars, enamels water,
makes the air and us giddy with light.

And once, at dawn—waterspouts—
muscular winds stir the emptiness
until it relents and raises watery arms
up into the clouds.

We smell the storm before it comes:
fresh, raw and damp. Its low, dark
ceiling rolls over us. We chase
the light until we catch the day before.

All too soon, a shape browns
on the horizon, hurling birds to meet us.

We dock in an assault of strange smells
and foreign faces—emerge
on rubbery legs, arms waving
like antennae, scanning the air
of yet another place I won't
want to leave.

Blood Brothers

—for Nan Hoskins

Every Saturday at the matinee, a lone man
took action, saved a town or wagon train
then rode away into next week's episode.
He outdrew, outshot or outsmarted
outlaws, gunslingers, cattle thieves and crooks.
With few words, he dealt justice
to a corrupt sheriff, a greedy rancher,
put backbone into the drunken judge
or cowardly dry-goods merchant and became
blood brother to an Apache chief.
His horse understood him best.

But women always cried, even the tough ones
in the saloon. The weaker sex got all weepy
when captured and again when rescued or
were sure to take some notion that the cowboy
was more than just friends then be all misty-eyed
when he left. We knew: tears sapped strength.
They were bad water, worse than the salty spring
the cowboy warned against—give in,
just once, and you were doomed.

Lizzie and I made our pact:
took the sharpest knife from the kitchen drawer,
decided our knees would be best
since they were the most used to bleeding.
Lizzie still had the hard purple streaks
her bike'd gouged down her shin and my scabs
weren't healed from the fence last week.

                    We couldn't make
the determined slice we'd seen on screen,
so scraped a little at a time, fuzzy

white to naked pink, until the skin was raw
and seeping. We pressed knee to knee,
repeated solemn words we'd heard cowboys
use and then the secret ones they didn't say
out loud: *We'll never cry, no matter what.*

We wiped the knife, hid the red Kleenex
in the bottom of the trash and went outside
to wait for Momma to come back and drive us—
out to the stables for the riding lessons
we'd won at the matinee.
Like finding sweet water.
I imagine a pinto for you
and a gray for me.

Objects at an Exhibition

Ruins
Every day one August a moped buzzes into Knossos and parks. The once-deep harbor is gone, shallowed by insistent seas. City too fell and rose...and fell again. Ground gave way. Waves—now gentle— lap its ruins. The rider, as she does each morning, dismounts to stand staring at the massive stucco horns that jut into the vault of Crete's summer-washed sky.

Fishermen and Sponge Divers
Somewhere off the highway in a bar near Tarpon Springs, sun-bitten Greeks put down drinks and take a place on the scuffed wooden floor. Hands clasped behind their backs, men dance like supplicating birds: strut, sway, lean, straighten, bend again and...smile. *Divers*, says the bartender, *found new beds, big ones, healthy, too. We'll all thank the saints come Sunday, but this goes way back, to when gods were mad...*

Lentoid Seal Stone, circa 1500 B.C.E.
Legs flying like the falling-man's silhouette on signs that warn of slippery rocks, a bull-leaper, flung into the air, clings to one horn, while a second figure lies crumpled under hooves that are at this moment, all off the ground. *The one on top in flight as his unsuccessful colleague is trampled,* or so the caption says.

Ivory Figurine with Gold Accents
This, I recognize—a slim, muscular acrobat (tense, poised, arm raised) signaling ready—and half-expect the single, plosive syllable heard, even at practice, from riders who stand on horseback as they stack and unstack, the abrupt burst of sound a beat before a taut body flips from the rump of a galloping mare onto the shoulders of a catcher who stands, knees unlocked, on the horse galloping behind.

Bronze Statuette
In fragments, the bronze is less clear—a somersaulter in motion, suspended between the horns of a bull, its head thrown up and back, angry momentum that may carry her past danger.

Minoan Frescoes
One, though *questionably restored*, is festive: a group of three with prancing bull—two girls positioned to catch or help (it's hard to tell) and a graceful boy, halfway through his cartwheel over the animal's back. In the audience: russet-skinned men and three women, white in bright dresses with dark, wavy, jewel-strung hair piled high and half-falling onto their dainty shoulders.

Agate Seal, circa 1600 B.C.E.
Bull charges over barricade, gores flailing figure—an emblem, made to be reproduced, stamped into clay or wax, to authenticate, signify, endorse. But who would want this brand? Olive oil *Approved by* also-rans. Official attar of failed bull dancers. Souvenir? Award? Guild badge? Strange—like a pilot's patch with crashed airplane and lifeless flyer or rodeo buckle with thrown cowboy under bucking bronco. The caption is noncommittal.

A Book of Myths: Index
Artifacts. Bulls—in games, sacrifices. Horns—of *obvious ritual significance*. As if that explained it. Minos—retribution of: (his Minotaur ate Athenians, seven youths and seven maidens every nine years). Ariadne—half-sister to the Minotaur; Minoan princess; goddess; and Theseus. Theseus—and bull-jump games (but that's another story)...and heroic deeds (slew the Marathon bull, sacrificed it to Apollo, angered Poseidon again)... Poseidon—god of earthquakes, tidal waves and bulls. Well, here's Zeus with at least one bull. None of it helps. Why preserve failure?

Back to the Seals
Why carved in stone? A warning? A message? For Cretans? Greeks? The world? Maybe tufted erect penis on goring bull signifies something that should be remembered; or *in flight* not to forget that no one can ever control his own life. A keepsake? Token. Of what? And those towering horns—portals aligned to stars? Do they open the sky? Point to fate? Remind us of the way the young, or anyone for that matter, is thrown into future unknown...if they're lucky?

Poppy Fields and Veteran

On stems so slender they disappear, wildflowers
float, purple a mist above white, yellow, gold
and blue bending together, snapping like white
caps in waves of fluorescent orange poppies.

Color that can't be remembered even if you try,
he says. *Oh, you can close your eyes,*
phosphorescence bursts, blazes again,
but nothing like sun-bright flares on the retinas
of open eyes—neurons firing and firing, until
stunned sight stops, shimmering...shimmering...

Like these after-images? I ask, still looking
at the backs of my eyelids, thinking I understand.

No, there's no after, just ... snow-blind with color.

Love in Another Tongue

— with apologies to Guy Deutscher

His poems spoke a forest of words, of dark-toed trees,
where nouns flicker like fireflies and verbs shriek bat-
like between the white-space meadows. If asked, he'd
say he was drawn to nature as a mode of expressing
love. And who can argue whether hoarfrost heckles?
After all, *thrilled* comes from pierced, as surely as arrows
find their mark and *sarcastic*, too, from cutting into flesh,
tearing skin. Grinding the arks, the arcs, the pelvic arches
of ancestral language, he wrung words into crinkled flowers,
into irregular hell-bent buds. It's all body—the stones of love,
bones becoming trumpets or flutes, moonlit coins, erotic
as ingots in vaulted rooms built from *God-Loves-You* figurines,
and of course the swimming pool's indigenous blondes.

Her poems wanted to speak only in vowels— ah, eh, oh, uh—
before slipping underwater to cavort with consonants in nonskid
aqua-socks. That's not to say she hadn't known derivations
of minx or vixen, the connotations of foxes, the wreaked
affinities in skink, skank, skunk, the rogue animal/vegetable
music mesh of skanking on a balcony, veranda, portico, lanai,
porch or stoop. Still, love worried her ear. Yeses elusive as
elixirs lurked like dawn behind the mountains over her
blackwater lakes. I write about that, she'd say when asked—
and the way in dreams, wishes rush down the blue rivers of my
arms, into the blue washes of my hands to bleach like minnows
in the sun.

> But well-behaved cases had already started to rot. Little
> by little, mouths lost ablatives, grew sore in love's
> datives: Her? Him? You gave to…?   Hither, whither,
> nothing whatsoever, not a wit. Hear-eth me?
> Be-eth you? Catapulted, then, ignited, erratic, accusative:
> I love you.   Yes loveth you I—it's heaven sent

moved to the nominative
you love me?   you say you love me
and finally genitive
was it mine, your love?
But in all its cases,
your love is breadcrumbs, fishbone, pea pod.

As the linguist explains, "Consider what happened to the phrase
Persian apple with its five juicy vowels and seven luscious
consonants…[only to end up] as a rather shriveled *peach*."

Butterfly Instrumental in Pismo Beach

Colorless in the damp
chill of early gray light

long clumps of monarchs
hang from branches

of eucalyptus and pine
till sun

in thin shafts
excites the air

like a conductor's baton
beginning to stir the flutes.

Struck by light
a few release their hold

and drift down,
prelude of mournful notes.

But then
the body trembles

gives way to clouds of fire,
crescendo of gold wings

together, apart
rising up

through the trees
as with one urge.

Some desire
like a phantom ache

resonates my dense
wingless body.

Mariano Zaro

Mariano Zaro is the author of four bilingual books
of poetry, most recently *The House of Mae Rim/La
casa de Mae Rim*. His poems appear in the anthologies
Monster Verse (Penguin Random House), *Wide Awake;
Poets of Los Angeles and Beyond* (Pacific Coast Poetry
Series 2015), and in several magazines in Spain,
Mexico, and the United States. Zaro has translated
American poets Tony Barnstone and Philomene Long.
He hosts a series of video interviews with prominent
poets for the literary project Poetry.LA.

Zaro earned a Ph.D. in Linguistics (University of Granada,
Spain) and a Master's in Literature (University of Zaragoza,
Spain). He is a Spanish professor at Rio Hondo College
(Whittier, CA).

Figs

I planted this fig tree the day you were born,
my father tells me.
The tree is tall, abundant, with dense shade.
It's my twin brother.

When in season, I bring figs to friends and neighbors.
Figs organized in concentric circles,
on a tray that my mother lines with fig leaves.
I also bring figs to my Uncle Santiago.
Don't knock at his front door, go through the garage,
my father says. My mother does not put the figs
on the tray, she puts them inside a paper bag.
My uncle Santiago is diabetic.
You are killing him. He cannot eat figs, his wife says.
I deliver the figs through the garage.
He is waiting. *Thank you for the contraband,* he says.
He gives me a coin, kisses the top of my head.
He eats the figs right there, in the garage,
without turning the lights on.
He opens the figs' skin with his thumbnail.

My Uncle Santiago is not my uncle. We call him uncle because
he grew up with my father.
My grandmother breastfed both of them.
And somehow they look alike, my father and Santiago—
tall, soft grey eyes, quiet.

Your fig tree is sick, my father says one summer.
He also says the word *fungus.*

The tree looks normal but when you turn the leaves
you can see little white spots, in clusters.
I go with my father to the pharmacy,
we buy some kind of powder, my father mixes it with water.

We cannot spray the tree now, it's too hot, my father says.
We have to wait until the sun goes down.

After we spray, the tree leaves start dripping—
a small, toxic rain that hits the ground. *Stay away*, my father says.
I ask, *Is the tree dying?*
Everything that breathes is dying, he says.

Could we plant another tree? I ask.
We could, but it takes a long time until it bears fruit.
Years. You will plant your trees one day, my father says.
My limbs feel heavy. I press my arms alongside my body.
I want to go home. Hide.
I don't want my father to wait in vain.

Red Swimsuits

We all wear red swimsuits
in this summer camp on the Mediterranean.
It's the rule, the uniform.
That way we are more visible
to the counselors taking care of us.
They are not really counselors,
they are still in college.

We swim on the beach.
It's so hot, the seagulls don't move.
Don't move on top of rocks,
on top of telephone poles.
We go back to the locker room,
we undress, we take a shower.
Today I cannot untie my swimsuit.
I have been in the water until the last minute.
The string is too wet, too tight.
I call one of the counselors.
He is tall.
All adults are tall when you are nine.
He tries the knot,
has big hands.
All adults have big hands.
It is too tight, he says.
He leans over
and unties the string with his teeth.
I feel his stubble against my belly,
for a second. Sandpaper, amber, mint,
danger in the border of flesh and fabric.
Go, hit the shower, he says.

I cannot move.
I lift my arms between crucifix and butterfly.
I lean against the lockers;
the metal doors rattle.

I see small, soft seagulls coming out of my chest.
Turquoise seagulls, aqua seagulls
that fly fast and hit the ceiling.
They scream, turn, open their beaks;
other seagulls come out of their mouths,
pink seagulls with red eyes.
Their wings on my throat,
on my eyelashes.

Finally, they find the narrow window,
they leave the room.

I am alone, the last one there.
From outside, somebody calls my name.
There is salt on the roof of my mouth.

On Being Jewish, Perhaps

The staircase is L-shaped
with a huge cactus in the corner.
Be careful with that,
my mother says every time
we go to visit my aunt Pepa.
Today we are there
because her son has died.

Her son was away, in college.
He wanted to be a lawyer but
liked music most of all.
He died suddenly, they say.

Everybody is in the kitchen,
my aunt and the neighbors,
all women, dressed in black.
My mother is not,
she didn't have time to change.

My aunt Pepa is sitting in a low chair,
she looks smaller than ever.
My mother and my aunt are cousins,
I believe. They hug, cry, don't really talk.
My mother grabs my arm,
brings me closer to my aunt.
I kiss her. She is cold, the air is cold.
A neighbor brings a couple of chairs.
He was so young, somebody says.
Nobody knows how he died.
We sit down.

The kitchen smells like bleach.
There is no food around.
This is the first time I see
the kitchen like this—
so clean, empty,

all pans and pots
put away in the cupboards,
no fruit in the fruit bowl,
no dish in the dish rack,
no bread.

I look at my mother.
Where is the body, I want to say.
My mother leans over,
whispers in my ear.
He is in the hospital.
They have to do an autopsy.
Somehow my aunt hears us
and she breaks down
and sobs as if the word autopsy
was even worse than the word death.

I notice that the TV is covered
with a white tablecloth,
so is the large mirror over the credenza.
The mirror is a sailboat.
More neighbors come.

What is an autopsy? I ask my mother
as soon as we leave the house.
They cut you open, they look inside
and then they sew you back together
with long stitches as if they don't care,
as if they all were in a rush, she says.
She stops and fixes the scarf
around my neck. *This wind*, she says.
What about the mirror? I say.
Oh, the neighbors did that, she says.
It's because of the sadness.

Plums

My father wraps plums
with newspapers.
I cut the pages in half.
He wraps the plums.
We are in the attic.
It's summer.
We don't talk.

He rolls the fruit,
his fingers twist both ends of the paper.
It's raining outside.
The plums look like wrapped candy.

He is meticulous, not too meticulous, just enough.

The plums have to be without nicks or cuts,
firm, not too ripe, unblemished.

The storms have been coming all afternoon.
That's why my father is home;
he couldn't go to the fields.

He ties the plums with a thin string,
like a necklace.
Five plums in each string, exactly five.
I don't know why.
His hands inspect the fruit, twist the paper,
tie the knots, do the math.
I hide my hands under the newspapers.

He is on a ladder now.
He hangs the strings from a wooden beam in the ceiling.
I pass the strings to him.
One by one.
Sometimes, unintentionally,
my hand brushes his hand.

He leans his body against the ladder,
rests for a moment,
cleans his sweat.
My father is old.

The strings dangle from the ceiling.
Plums in-waiting like dull,
modest Christmas ornaments.

Fruit for the winter, he says.
As if you could wrap the summer with newspapers.
As if you could wrap your father's hands
for the future days of hunger.

The Actress

María Elena eats a yogurt a day,
low fat, not at once. And little more.
Some baby carrots, perhaps,
a rice cake.
Eating makes me dirty.
But people don't know
that I am always hungry.
This is what she told me once,
between rehearsals.

We are in the same theater class.
We rehearse in the evenings
and all day Saturdays
in a warehouse
that used to be a furniture store.

She comes late, María Elena.
She still has one third of the yogurt,
intact, in the container.
She closes the lid with Scotch tape
so she can carry the yogurt in her purse.
She also carries a white plastic spoon
and her baby carrots.
Because of all the carrots she eats
the skin of her hands is turning orange,
pale orange, not the whole skin,
that line where the palm becomes
the back of your hand,
that perimeter.

Sometimes María Elena sucks the empty spoon,
when she is distracted, looking away.
She has sunken cheeks,
that thing that looks so good in the movies.

She is Neighbor #1 in a play by Lorca,
the pregnant neighbor.
She refuses to wear the small,
round pillow under her dress.
I think the director has given up on that.

She also has a short monologue,
and at the end,
you can hear the effort
of her breathing, when she inhales,
you can see the veins on her neck,
the pasty white saliva,
the thick hairs on her arms
against the light,
the ribs through the fabric.
She has no breasts.

When she is finished
she puts on her coat,
tightens the belt
around her waist,
looks inside her purse,
lies down on an old couch,
and falls asleep.

I wake her up
when the rehearsal is over—
her arm on her face,
at an angle,
the plastic spoon
on the floor
covered with teeth marks.

The Card Player

I go with my mother to the nursing home
to visit some of her friends.
She wears her navy blue suit, and a pearl necklace.
The pearls are large and irregular,
deep gray on the verge of purple.
For a woman of ninety, the necklace is almost too daring.

It's late June, everybody sits at two big tables
near the garden. Women sit together, men sit together.
That's the way it is. Nobody sits outside.
Too much of a risk, they say, don't ever trust the weather.

My mother sits at the women's table.
They all talk at the same time.
Somebody mentions my mother's necklace.
They ask questions. They don't wait for answers.
They list illnesses, symptoms,
names of people who died recently.
They do the math; the years since the husbands died.
Already twenty years, my mother says.
At one point the table gets quiet; some women fall asleep,
or they just close their eyes.

My mother walks to the men's table.
They are playing cards. One of them turns his chair
and places his cards, face down, on top of the green felt.
He is not facing the table now; he is facing my mother.
Then, he says, *That's a nice necklace you are wearing.*
At the same time, he opens his legs.

There is nothing strange about it.
A man sitting on a chair opens his legs.
But my mother covers her necklace with her left hand.
She talks to the other men, she laughs.
They stop the game for a moment.
She does not sit with them. She says goodbye.
She keeps her hand on top of the necklace
until we leave the room.

The Philosopher

When we go to his apartment
there is a girl sleeping at the door,
curled up like a dog.
Not tonight, sweetie, he tells her,
I have company.

She leaves without a word.
I am the company.

We met long ago
at a birthday party.
He was my friend Clara's boyfriend,
he was also an assistant professor,
the youngest,
in the Philosophy department.
They made a great couple together,
he and Clara.
They were beautiful
without trying,
beautiful when tired, when dirty,
under the wrong light.

Too many girls, my friend told me
when they broke up.

Today we run into each other
in a bar where he used to go
with Clara. And we talk.
He talks in that voice that
tells you *Hey, you are the only one here.*
A voice made of walnuts
and secrecy and surrender.

We play the syllogism game,
the one we played with Clara,
always starting with

Socrates is a man,
all men are mortal,
therefore, Socrates is mortal.
He wants to try something else, he says.
Some stones become birds,
a canary is a bird,
therefore, some canaries are stones.

You just tell me where
you want me to stop.
This is the first thing I say
when we are both
inside the apartment.

He takes me to the window.
Look, he says.
You see these balconies?
The window faces an inner patio.
People enclose the balconies,
with glass panels.
They gain, how much?
Five more square feet
for the living room,
for one more chair.
They work hard for one more chair.

I kiss him because that is
what I have to do, what I want to do.
And I look at him and he looks
at his reaction and he undresses—
no underwear.
I notice that his apartment
is really dirty, with worn-out furniture,
that the curtain rail hangs uneven
like a broken arm.

His sex is dark, darker
than the rest of his body,
foreign against the pale
frame of the hips.
It's also luminous and crisp
like an unopened morning.

*Your chest is hard,
it's full of ribs*, he says,
when we are in bed.
And then he faces down,
all stretched like a board.
*Turn a little, it's easier
if you are on your side,* I say.
He turns but the body is too tight,
and I become a useless locksmith
of fingertips and saliva.

*Socrates is a man,
all men are mortal*, I say.
He says, *Therefore Socrates is mortal.*
And there, when he says *Socrates,*
in that last "s" his body opens
and I go in without pushing
or moving, nothing.

I rest my forehead on his neck,
the back of his neck.
Son of a bitch, he says.
We run, we think we run,
without touching the floor.
We run in a dense forest
with tall, violent ferns,
ferns as tall as we are
tall as fighting bears
or horses.

We are hit by branches,
pine needles, brambles,
we have lacerations,
apertures for air and mud
in the flesh,
for one more forest.

The next day the light wakes me up
but he is not there. He is sitting
in the kitchen, naked, with his legs up on a chair,
the ankles crossed,
the sex smooshed between the thighs,
skin tense, with thin violet veins,
more a tumor than a fruit.

I made some coffee, he says,
but there is nothing to eat,
some ice cream, maybe.
I want to say, let me go out
to get some pastries, but I don't.
He is reading something,
correcting papers.
I drink my coffee.
He turns a page.

Acknowledgments

We are grateful to the editors and publishers of the following journals, anthologies, and books in which these poems (sometimes in earlier versions or under different titles) previously appeared:

Marjorie Becker

- "Durham, 1980." *Desde Hong Kong: Poets in conversation with Octavio Paz on the occasion of the poet's centenary* (Hong Kong: Chameleon Press, 2010)
- "The Man Who Danced me in Spain" and "Body Bach." *Body Bach* (Tebot Bach, 2005)
- "Since Anything Can Always Always." *Chaparral* (2010)
- "Internal Hum" and "Painless Tattoo of Song." *Piano Glass/Glass Piano* (Tebot Bach, 2010)
- "Respect So Raw, So Real." *Spillway* (v.22, Muse and Music)
- "His tricks undid the inner light" and "Notes on Coupling." *Askew* (v.17, 2015)

Jeanette Clough

- "Evocation." *Colorado Review* (Spring 2014)
- "Memory," *Cider Press Review* (2006), and "Quiet," *Colorado Review* (Spring 2007), and "Salt," *Steam Ticket: A Third Coast Review* (Spring 2012). All three, plus "Acoustic Rain," *Flourish* (Tebot Bach Press, 2013).
- "Letter from Atlantis 2" (as "First Shudder"), *Denver Quarterly* (Spring/Summer 2001), and "Raga 6," *Wisconsin Review* (v35, #3, 2001). Both, plus "Leaving Palm Springs," *Island* (Red Hen Press 2007).
- "Here." *The Laurel Review* (v.47, 2014)
- "Coloratura." *Spillway* (v.20, 2013)
- "Tracking." *Spillway* (v.22, 2014)
  Note: "Acoustic Rain" emerged from *Rainforest IV*, an interactive electroacoustic environment conceived by David Tudor in 1973. The 2001 version was a project of the Getty Research Institute, Los Angeles, and realized by Composers Inside Electronics of California Institute of the Arts. The sound sculpture was presented at the CalArts Disney Modular Theater on May 17, 2001. (from Program Notes)

Dina Hardy

- "[Elsewhere scrims of light]," "[In the Natural History of Projection & Bone]" and "[Fallen black figs]." *Birds Piled Loosely* (#8, 2016) Nicole Letson, Johnathan McClintick, Karolina Zapal, eds.
- "the magician's assistant." *Gulf Coast.* (v.28, #2, 2016). Martin Rock, ed.
- "On the Island of the Fire Eaters [have you heard]." *Fanzine* (2014). Molly Brodak, guest ed.
- "On the Island of the Fire Eaters [we burn books and eat]." *Prelude* (2016). Stu Watson, ed.
- "corona." *21 Love Poems.* Hells Yes Press. Brad Liening, ed. (2012)
- "A Brief History of Razors and Shaving." *Southest Review*, (v.28 #1, 2010) Poetry contest finalist. Julianna Baggott, contest judge
- "A Prediction." *Lo-Ball* (#3). D.A. Powell, T. J. Difranceso, eds.
- "Yours Is Everything." *H_NGM_N* (#18, 2016). Nate Pritts, ed.
- "letters from the land of white pith helmets & puggarees." *decomP magazinE* (2016). Jason Jordan, ed.
- "Tomorrow, I'll climb a mountain." *Ink Brick* (v.5, 2016). Alexander Rothman, ed.
- "On the Island of the Fire Eaters [the flicker of death]." *Florida Review* (v.35, #2, 2010). Lisa Roney, ed.
- "Dinwiddie   pg. 1996   Diphtheria." *Selections from The World Book.* (Convulsive Editions, 2012). Nathan Hoks and Nicole Flores, eds.; *Transom* (Issue 1, 2011). Kiki Petrosino and Dan Rosenberg, eds.
- "Little Jesus." *Burnside Review* (v.4.1, 2008) "The L.A. Issue." Sid Miller, ed.

Paul Lieber

- "Los Angeles." Allen Ginsberg Contest, Honorable Mention winner. *Paterson Literary Review* (Issue 40, 2012-2013)
- "Off Broadway," *Poemeleon* and "The First Blackout." *Chemical Tendencies* (Tebot Bach, 2011)
- "Another Ocean Poem." *California Quarterly* (2016)
- "Homesick." Gival Press, LLC

Sarah Maclay

- "28 There was her method of swooning." *Taos Journal of Poetry and Art* (Fall 2013)
- "29 But there was another subject." *Mentalshoes_015* (2010)
- "4 —*as, after Odysseus, her body wanted to be Ophelia.*" *Superstition Review* (Fall 2012) and *Wide Awake; Poets of Los Angeles and Beyond* (Pacific Coast Poetry Series 2015)
- "7 Because identity had gone" and "31 —*Mystery Box.*" *Superstition Review* (Fall 2012)
- All five above: *The "She" Series: A Venice Correspondence* (What Books Press, 2016), a braided collaboration with Holaday Mason.
- "Woman Chained to Fire." *Poetry International* (2005), *Beyond the Lyric Moment* (Tebot Bach, 2014), and *Life and Legends. Issue 1.* (Summer 2014)
- "Leaves." *The American Poetry Review.* (November 2006)
- "Grille." *FIELD* (#72, Spring 2005), *Wide Awake; Poets of Los Angeles and Beyond* (Pacific Coast Poetry Series 2015), *The Write Question* (Montana Public Radio—KUFM, Nov. 16, 2015), and Pushcart Special Mention in *Pushcart Prize Anthology XXXI.* .
- All three above: *The White Bride* (U of Tampa Press, 2008)
- "Night Text." *FIELD.* (#91, Fall 2014) and *Poetry Daily* (Nov. 15, 2014)
- "Girl Standing with Death by the Sea." *Fanzine* (Feb. 20, 2015)

Holaday Mason

- "Wolves Drawn to The Sound of Bells," *Talking River Review* (2002) and "Reciting the Water." *Poetry International* (2002), and "Power." *The Greensboro Review* (2005). All three: *Towards The Forest* (New Rivers Press, 2007)
- "The Boy is The Man I Loved." *Pedestal Magazine* (2015)
- "Paris, day 2." *The Taos Literary Review* (2015)
- "Old Music." *Apercus Quarterly* (2016)
- "As Satie Winds Up The Stairs." *Pool* (2008)
- W"32 I took you inside," "31 Twisting, we smell of wet horses/salt/granite," and "1 The book is still." *The "She" Series: A Venice*

Correspondence (What Books Press, 2016), a braided collaboration with Sarah Maclay
- "Mid Point Mercury Retrograde." *Apercus Quarterly* (2016)
- "That Jacaranda, Ten Years Old this August" and "Portrait of Child With Mask." *Spillway* (2015)
- "Inside The Radio." *So Luminous the Wildflowers* (Tebot Bach, 2003)

Jim Natal
- "Windchime Tantra." *Yalobusha Review*; *In the Bee Trees* (Archer Books, 2000)
- "What They Do," *Poets for Peace* and "Rest Area." *NoHo LA.*; *Talking Back to the Rocks* (Archer Books, 2003)
- "Borderline." *Mischief, Caprice, and Other Poetic Devices* (Red Hen Press, 2004), "Lost: One-Footed Adult Crow. Reward." Open Windows Arroyo Arts Collective (2005), "Photographic Memory: II." *Bellingham Review,* and "In Memory of Her Memory: IV." *Beyond Forgetting: Poetry and Prose About Alzheimer's Disease* (Kent State University Press, 2009). All four, plus "Rain in L.A.: Saturday Sunset." *Memory and Rain* (Red Hen Press, 2009)
- "Underwater" and "My student writes." *52 Views: The Haibun Variations* (Tebot Bach, 2013)
- "After Paris in December." *Hayden's Ferry Review*
- "Jesus, St. Anthony, St. Simeon on His Pillar." *Alligator Juniper*
- "Gratitude (The Gospel According to Arnie's Accountant)." *Spillway*

Jan Wesley
- "Double Exposure." *Lumina Magazine*
- "My Old Man Gets Sick and Dies and Leaves this Hole in the Universe." Pushcart Nominee. *Iowa Review*
- "First Boy." Poetry contest finalist, *The Comstock Review*
- "Duets for the End of Time" *Psychological Perspectives – Los Angeles Jung Institute*

Brenda Yates

- "The Universe's Clock." *Mercury Retrograde* (Kattywompus Press, 2013)
- "Demarcations." *Blueline* (v.XXXVII, 2016)
- "Seven Ways of Reckoning." Robinson Jeffers Tor House Foundation 2014 Poetry Prize Announcements; *Tor House Newsletter* (Summer 2014)
- "Melancholy Anagrams." *Spillway* (v.14, Tebot Bach, 2010)
- "Martini II." *Sliver of Stone Magazine* (Issue 10, 2015)
- "Another Place I Don't Want to Leave." *Naugatuck River Review* (Issue 14, 2015)
- "Blood Brothers." *Manifest West* (Western Press Books, 2013) "Even Cowboys Carry Cell Phones" issue
- "Objects at an Exhibition." *Illuminations 29: An International Magazine of Contemporary Writing* (Rathasker Press, 2013)
- "Poppies and Veteran." *Brain of Forgetting* (Issue II, Brain of Forgetting Press, Cork, Ireland, 2015) "Poppies" issue
- "Love in Another Tongue." *Askew* (v.12, 2012)
- "Butterfly Instrumental in Pismo Beach." *Mason's Road* (Issue 10, 2014)

Mariano Zaro

- "Figs." *Pinyon* (2016)
- "Red Swimsuits." *Wide Awake; Poets of Los Angeles and Beyond.* (Pacific Coast Poetry Series, 2015)
- "On Being Jewish, Perhaps." *Zócalo Public Square* (2014)
- "Plums." *Tupelo Quarterly* (2013)
- "The Card Player." *River's Voice* (2010)
- "The Philosopher." *The New Guard* (2016)